One Step at a Time

A structured programme for teaching spoken language in nurseries and primary schools

Ann Locke

with Don Locke

Published by Network Continuum Education
The Tower Building, 11 York Road, London SE1 7NX

An imprint of The Continuum International Publishing Group

www.networkcontinuum.co.uk
www.continuumbooks.com

First published 2006
© Ann Locke 2006

ISBN-13:   978 1 85539 117 8
ISBN-10:   1 85539 117 1

Managing editor: Margaret Finn
Design by: Neil Hawkins, Network Continuum Education
Cover design by: Neil Hawkins, Network Continuum Education
Proofreader: Lynn Bresler

Printed in Great Britain by Ashford Colour Press, Gosport, Hants

Contents

Introduction

One Step at a Time is the product of more than 40 years, during which I have been, variously, a speech and language therapist, teacher, educational psychologist, support service adviser, and university researcher and lecturer, thinking about and working with children who seem to be having difficulty acquiring and using spoken language. Over that time my interests and focus have changed, as have the issues we need to confront, but one constant thread has been my belief that the only way to deal with these problems effectively is through the school system. It is only by using classroom and nursery teaching staff that we can provide the degree of contact and support and the amount of repetition and reinforcement that children need if they are to acquire the language skills necessary to make progress in school and beyond.

My first project (*Living Language*, 1985) was a detailed language-teaching programme for children with moderate to severe learning difficulties. It was intended for use in special schools and units with children who had barely begun to talk; it dealt with only the most basic language skills, and required intensive adult intervention. It was clearly not a model for wider classroom use in either special or mainstream schools.

During the late 1980s there was a growing awareness of the number of children in mainstream schools whose spoken language was inadequate for the demands of the recently introduced National Curriculum. At the same time, children with special educational needs were being integrated into mainstream education, and support services were becoming stretched to the point where they could not always provide the specialist support and advice that teachers might need to work with these children.

Teaching Talking (1991, second edition 2005), co-written with Maggie Beech, attempted to remedy this. It provides ways for classroom teachers to identify and work with children whose language development is delayed for their age, beginning with relatively low-level classroom intervention but providing more intensive intervention for those children who need it. It anticipated and is now integrated with the *Special Educational Needs Code of Practice* (DfES 1994, revised 2001) with its three-tier approach of initial identification, 'Action' and 'Action Plus' intervention. But *Teaching Talking* is primarily a programme for children with special educational needs, broadly defined, and provides the detailed assessment and close personal intervention that many of these children need. It too does not provide a model for whole-class mainstream intervention.

By the late 1990s the major problem was becoming the number of children entering schools and nurseries with extremely limited spoken language, especially in areas of economic deprivation and social disadvantage. This was partly because more children were entering nursery at an age when they would still be developing basic spoken language skills, but there also seemed to be many more children with impoverished spoken language, perhaps as a result of cultural factors. By the end of the decade, language delay had even been identified as the most common childhood disability (Law, Parkinson and Tamhe, 2000).

At the same time the school curriculum had become increasingly focused on literacy and numeracy. To a considerable extent, schools were being judged, formally and informally, on how soon they introduced children to literacy, and how many children they managed to get to an acceptable standard of reading and writing by the ages of 7 or 11. But children with seriously delayed or impoverished spoken language were not in a position to respond to this pressure and, as a result, the Literacy Strategy met with mixed success, especially in deprived and disadvantaged areas.

We have to be able to walk before we can run and, except for some special cases, we have to be able to talk before we can read or write. If children are not fluent in spoken language it is a great deal more difficult for them to become fluent in reading and writing. Instead of being introduced to literacy as soon as possible, many children needed work on the underlying language skills that make literacy possible. And this does not apply only to literacy. The ability to understand and use spoken language fluently is the basis of all learning and is essential for progress at school as well as for personal and social development.

It has always seemed to me that our education system takes spoken language too much for granted, in policy and in practice, in the curriculum and in the classroom, in advice and guidance and in teacher training. In some parts of the country the majority of children entering schools and nurseries have inadequate spoken language for the demands of the early years curriculum. Schooling, especially with younger children and in areas of deprivation and disadvantage, needs to start with the essential spoken language skills that make learning, literacy and personal development possible.

However, this problem was too big to be dealt with by an intensive support programme such as *Living Language* or *Teaching Talking*. They are too demanding of staff time to be used with significant numbers of children in a primary classroom. Staff are in any case already under too much pressure from other curriculum initiatives and demands to give much thought or attention to spoken language, particularly as this is, through no fault of their own, an area in which they mostly lack training or expertise.

So it seemed to me that I needed to find a different, more practicable approach to spoken language teaching, one that could be whole-class, all-needs and manageable in primary schools and nurseries. From my experience of working with an Education Action Zone in Sheffield I realized that the programme should start not so much with the needs of children as with the needs of staff. To benefit the children – even to reach the children who need it – a spoken language programme has to be manageable by classroom staff within existing resources and the current curriculum, and without the benefit of specialist training or expert support.

The solution lay in a curriculum model in which spoken language teaching supports and grows out of the rest of the school curriculum, showing teachers what to teach, and when and how to teach it in the course of everyday lessons and daily classroom activities. What is also required is a structured approach that staff can implement one step at a time, enabling children to learn one step at a time. The name of the programme began to seem inevitable.

One Step at a Time arose originally from my experience with a piece of applied research in a Sheffield Education Action Zone, and has since been trialled to varying degrees in several places, most notably in Newport, South Wales. The Newport project is now in its fifth year and includes 21 nurseries and primary schools, with more joining every year. I have worked very closely with both advisory and teaching staff and, as a result, the programme has changed and evolved as children have worked through it from the nursery at ages 3 to 4 to Year 2 at ages 6 to 7.

It is still too soon to evaluate the detailed effects on children's educational progress but some things are already apparent. One is that it can be done: the programme is manageable by existing staff within existing resources. It fits easily into existing planning and practice, and can be integrated with current teaching without adding appreciably to teachers' burdens. Another is that the programme is beneficial in increasing teachers' insight into children's spoken language, its development, complexity and structure, and their awareness of its importance for children's educational progress. Yet another is the programme's impact on children's confidence, not just in their willingness to talk and use spoken language but their willingness to 'have a go' in other areas, and especially in reading and writing. Boys in particular seem more willing to write about something if they have been able to talk about it first. *One Step at a Time* seems particularly effective with the slower children, who tend to get left behind, not just those who seem to be having difficulty with spoken language but others who seem destined for the now notorious 'tail of underachievement'.

But what has been most gratifying of all is the extremely positive response of staff: their enjoyment in using the programme and the enthusiasm with which they report children's involvement, interest and progress. *One Step at a Time* builds the confidence of staff as much as of children, and confidence, ultimately, is what it is all about: confidence in using spoken language, and confidence in teaching it.

Acknowledgements

One Step at a Time would not have been possible without the encouragement and support of a large number of people. Above all, I have to thank the schools and staff in Newport who made the project very much their own, and who did so much to shape and develop its final form. The project would not have been possible in the first place without the support, enthusiasm and sheer driving force of Dr Claire Watkins, a senior adviser with the Newport Local Education Authority. The headteachers of the first schools to use the programme – Jyothi Mathkar, Lesley Ilott, Lorraine Grange and Brenda Bispham – were also instrumental in getting the project off the ground and in carrying it through its first cycle. I owe them all a huge debt. I thank them too for their hospitality and friendship.

I have also benefited enormously from the comments, advice and suggestions of classroom staff. Their feedback on the content, implementation and manageability of the programme has been invaluable, and in several places I have learned as much from them as they, I hope, have learned from me. If I particularly mention Emma Jones, Catherine Place, Suzy Watkins, Sue Newman and Jenny Summers it may only be because they were in at the beginning and were able to offer advice and suggest improvements at the time when it was most needed.

Outside of Newport I would like to thank Margaret Booth and the schools and staff in the South East Sheffield Education Action Zone for their patience and support as I tried and tested some of my early ideas, and Faith Hobson and Chris Quinlan who have been responsible for introducing the *One Step at a Time* approach in Stoke-on-Trent as part of the *Stoke Speaks Out* project.

I also owe thanks to Sue Finn, Bridget Winn, and especially Maggie Beech for reading and commenting on the text and materials. Maggie's expert comments were detailed, constructive and thought-provoking, and the text is much improved as a result. My thanks, too, to Margaret Finn for her helpful and careful editing of the final text.

But my greatest debt must be to my husband, Professor Don Locke. This time it goes well beyond the usual acknowledgement of support, encouragement and forbearance. This book was written with him. Although he is not an educationalist or a language specialist, it has been very much a joint project.

We dedicate *One Step at a Time* to our children and grandchildren.

Ann Locke

How to use this book

One Step at a Time is divided into three main sections:

◆ *Background*: Chapters 1–4 provide the rationale for the *One Step at a Time* programme. They explain the importance of spoken language for children's development and their progress in school, and discuss three major problems that arise for teaching spoken language: the size and complexity of the spoken language system; the intensity of natural language learning; and the manageability of spoken language teaching in classroom settings.

◆ *Overview*: Chapters 5–8 introduce the programme and explain its structure and methodology, including its general procedures and school management issues.

◆ *Detailed procedures*: Chapters 9–13 give detailed procedures and advice on teaching methods and activities for each step of the programme.

Resource materials, which include initial screens, skills checklists and vocabulary wordlists, are included in each of the *Detailed procedures* chapters. They provide detailed teaching objectives and can be photocopied for use in the purchasing institution. *One Step at a Time* also suggests teaching activities but does not attempt to specify teaching materials because they are so vast and various and should be readily available, arising naturally out of the rest of the curriculum.

The first four chapters can be read independently of the *One Step at a Time* programme. They are intended for readers who want to know why spoken language matters and how the issue needs to be addressed.

The programme itself is summarized briefly in Chapter 5. Schools wishing to introduce *One Step at a Time* should also study Chapters 6–8 as background to the programme as a whole. However, they should also read Chapters 1–4, to understand why the programme is needed, and why it has been developed as it has.

Staff who are implementing *One Step at a Time* in the classroom will want to concentrate on the appropriate chapter in Chapters 9–13. But just as staff responsible for the programme as a whole should read Chapters 1–4 as background, so classroom staff should read Chapters 5–8 to see how their own step fits into the wider programme, and for general advice on procedures and teaching methods.

The reader who wants a brief introduction to *One Step at a Time* should begin with Chapter 5. It stands on its own and summarizes the main points from the earlier chapters. There is also significant overlap between Chapters 6 and 7, which describe general procedures and teaching methods, and Chapters 9–13, each of which gives detailed procedures and teaching methods for a specific step in the programme. This overlap and repetition is deliberate so that classroom staff can use one part of the programme without constantly having to refer to other chapters.

For the sake of simplicity, *One Step at a Time* has been written with reference to the English education system, with its terminology of key stages, Year 1 and Year 2, and so on. This is, of course, dispensable – *One Step at a Time* has been trialled in Wales, after all – and the relevant ages are provided to assist readers from other systems and other countries.

I have also, for the sake of clarity, adopted a convention with personal pronouns that adults are female and children are male. That is, teachers, parents and other adults are referred to as 'she', and children are referred to as 'he'. This convention has no hidden significance beyond the fact that the majority of early years staff are female.

List of photocopiable resource materials

The following materials may be photocopied for use in the purchasing institution.

Discussion skills

Appendix 2

1

Why spoken language matters

What is the single most important skill that children need for school, to think and learn, understand and communicate, read and write, ask and answer questions, negotiate, reason and problem solve, express their thoughts and feelings, establish friendships, co-operate with others and manage their own behaviour?

The answer, in a word, is language; in two words, spoken language. Except for some children with distinctive special needs, spoken language is the basic form of human communication and the principal method of teaching right through to further and higher education. Most of what goes on in classrooms involves talk. Without fluency in spoken language, without the ability to understand and respond, to ask as well as answer questions, children will not learn much from what happens in school.

Spoken language is crucial for:

◆ **teaching**
Most teaching is talking, especially in the early years. Teachers talk and children listen. Children have to understand what we say or they will learn nothing; and they have to respond to our talk for us to know what they have learned.

◆ **learning**
Children also learn by talking to us, by reformulating in their own words what we have told them or extending their learning by asking questions or suggesting further ideas of their own.

◆ **literacy**
Children need to be fluent in spoken language before they can become fluent in written language. They need to know the words when they read them or 'reading' becomes a mechanical exercise devoid of meaning; they need to know what to say and how to say it or 'writing' becomes the making of pointless marks on paper.

◆ **thinking**
Children need language to think with. We clarify our thoughts by finding words to express them, and more complex or sophisticated ideas require more complex or sophisticated language. Sentence structure, in particular, enables us to formulate complex ideas, for example about *what will happen because …* or *what might happen if …* .

◆ **social and emotional development**
Talk is a social skill. Children need to be able to communicate with other people to make friends, join in their activities and learn from them. Children who cannot talk easily or coherently may be isolated or bullied. They also need the language to explain how they are feeling or why they are behaving as they do, and to understand other people's behaviour as well as their own. Children who cannot express themselves, who cannot identify their own feelings, will be frustrated, difficult, perhaps aggressive.

The likelihood is that children entering school with limited spoken language will be significantly disadvantaged both through their schooling and later in life. Yet spoken language is not something that schools usually think of themselves as needing to teach. Speaking and listening are recognized as a key element in a broad and balanced curriculum along with art and design, music, health education and physical exercise. But they are not seen as fundamental, essential to all learning. That role is given instead to written language, even though written language can hardly develop without spoken language to build on.

The reason seems obvious. Literacy is recognized as something that schools need to teach; it is, in large part, what schools are there for. If there were no schools, most children would not learn to read and write. Spoken language, by contrast, is seen as something that children will learn at home and bring to school with them. It is taken for granted that they will come into school or nursery already equipped with the spoken language they need.

Increasingly, however, this is not the case. It was probably never wholly true. There will always have been some children whose spoken language was inadequate even for primary school. They will have been the children who were always behind, always struggling and who, as the years progressed, fell ever further behind. But there now seem to be many more of them.

This is not just a matter of special needs, though more children are now identified as having special educational needs than was previously the case. Nor is it a matter of children for whom English is an additional language, though there are more of these children too. It is more a matter of increasing numbers of children coming into school, especially from deprived or disadvantaged backgrounds, with inadequate spoken language. But it is not just social deprivation. There are cultural factors affecting all children: the decline in family meals around a dining table; the increased use of dummies to keep children quiet; pushchairs facing away from the adult instead of prams that faced towards them, so the pusher could chat with the baby; TV replacing or drowning out adult talk; adults talking on mobile phones while they feed their babies; unspillable beakers so children no longer have to ask for a drink; TVs in children's bedrooms; videos and computer games.

Schools are well aware of these issues. In 2001, 75 per cent of headteachers admitting three year olds were concerned about a decline in children's competence in spoken language (National Literacy Trust, 2001). In 2002 teachers in Wales reported talking and listening skills as the abilities that had most declined over the previous five years (Basic Skills Agency, 2002). In 2003 Ofsted inspectors were concerned about the speaking and listening skills of as many as half of four and five year olds starting school (TES, 2004). In 2004 89 per cent of nursery workers were worried about the growing occurrence of speech, language and communication difficulties among pre-school children including concentrating, speaking clearly, following instructions and responding with monosyllabic answers or gestures rather than appropriate language (ICAN, 2004). And these problems persist, through junior school and beyond. Children's language improves, naturally, but even at secondary school many students remain inarticulate, unable to express or explain themselves, unwilling or unable to communicate.

There are, moreover, other more complex skills that children need to develop at school. It has been calculated that while it takes immigrant children from non-English-speaking countries about two years to become fluent in conversational English, it takes between five and seven years for them to reach the level of spoken English needed for competent performance at school or in cognitive and reading tests (Cummins and Swain, 1986). These skills, too, get taken for granted. We assume that children whose home language is English will just pick them up by themselves, without targeted intervention, just as they picked up conversational English. But children whose language is already delayed when they enter school will find these more advanced skills even more difficult, and will steadily fall further and further behind.

Spoken language, disadvantage and attainment

Politicians and policy-makers do now acknowledge a link between social disadvantage and educational attainment. There was a time when it was seen as 'patronizing' to suggest that children from poorer homes might be unable to take the same advantage of education as middle-class children. But it is now accepted that children from deprived areas with higher initial ability actually do less well at school than children from middle-class backgrounds with lower initial ability. The less able children from wealthier homes overtake the more able, poorer children by the age of 6, and the gap between them 'explodes' in the early years of secondary school (DfES, 2004). The government itself now sees the failure to narrow this gap as the major failing in its educational strategy (Kelly, 2005). What politicians and policy-makers seem not to appreciate, however, are the intervening links between disadvantage and spoken language (Ginsborg, forthcoming), and between spoken language and educational attainment (Snow, 2001).

Studies in a deprived area of Sheffield showed that more than half the children entering nursery at ages 3 to 4 had spoken language that was noticeably delayed for their age, and almost 10 per cent had language that was severely delayed (Locke, Ginsborg and Peers, 2002). This was not a generalized delay – these children's cognitive scores were around average – but specific to language. Even more worryingly, when the same children were retested two years later their cognitive scores had improved but their language scores, relative to age, had not (Locke and Ginsborg, 2003). The total number showing some delay had decreased slightly, but the number whose language was now severely delayed, relative to age, had almost tripled! A few children had caught up, but many more were further behind than ever.

The link between spoken language and attainment can be illustrated by one of the key elements in the government's educational strategy, children's literacy. One minister of education promised to resign if the proportion of 11 year olds reaching an acceptable standard in reading and writing did not increase from just under half in 1997 to 80 per cent by 2002. This figure had still not been reached in 2005, so the ministry set itself a new target: 85 per cent by 2008. In the meantime one in five of our children is still leaving primary school without the skills needed to succeed in secondary school and beyond. In a fifth of schools it is one child in three. In the part of Sheffield mentioned above it remains one in two.

This should not be blamed on 'a stubborn core of persistently weak schools ... where children are not given chances in literacy' (DfES, 2004). It is not just schools that 'do not always seem to understand the importance of pupils' talk in developing both reading and writing' (Ofsted, 2005). Except for some special cases, children need to be competent in spoken language before they can become competent in written language. Ofsted's review of the English inspection evidence refers to research which argues that 'Spoken language forms a constraint, a ceiling not only on the ability to comprehend but also on the ability to write, beyond which literacy cannot progress' (Myhill and Fisher, 2005). It has been estimated that children with inadequate speech and language in the early years are up to six times more likely to experience reading problems in school (Boyer, 1991).

Yet at the same time that children are coming into education earlier and earlier, they are being put under greater pressure to read and to write. In other countries they do it differently, with better results (Alexander, 2000). Reading and writing are not introduced until children are 6 or 7. The early years are devoted instead to the systematic teaching of spoken language and other pre-literacy skills that children need to establish first. But in the United Kingdom schools are under pressure to introduce all children to reading and writing as early as possible. It is expected that most children will be doing some reading and writing by the end of the reception year (ages 4 to 5).

Most teachers know that many children entering school, especially from disadvantaged backgrounds, are simply not ready for literacy. They know that forcing them into reading and writing will be pointless and counter-productive: these children will not learn to read and write with any confidence; they will learn only to be failures. They also recognize that children who struggle to acquire the mechanics of literacy are only storing up problems for later: they may be able to read the words but they will not be able to read with understanding; they may be able to write the words but they will not be able to produce a coherent text. And even if they manage to make the grade at age 11, they will probably be out of their depth at secondary school. These children are doubly disadvantaged. They are disadvantaged when they enter school and they are disadvantaged by what happens there. They form that stubborn 'tail of underachievement' that is currently the cause of so much concern.

In fact, many children entering nursery, especially in deprived and disadvantaged areas, are not ready for formal teaching of any kind. Some are barely at the level of language development that might be expected of a two year old and will need a great deal of support and encouragement to develop the basic confidence and communication that are the foundation of all learning. Whenever children are slow to acquire an essential skill like spoken language, we need to do two things.

◆ We need to start much further back than might otherwise be the case, to ensure that these children are fully competent in the basic skills that make more advanced expertise possible. If they are not competent in the basic skills they will always have difficulty with the more complex skills that presuppose them.

◆ We need to provide much more in the way of practice, repetition, consolidation and generalization than might otherwise be the case, to ensure that these children have mastered these skills and are able to use them fluently, spontaneously and automatically.

Neither of these is easy in today's educational climate, where the pressure is always to move children on and produce results as quickly as possible. Staff are often aware that the curriculum they have to offer these children is inappropriate and counter-productive, but have no clear idea of what to put in its place and little encouragement to try a different approach.

Giving priority to spoken language

Impoverished spoken language doesn't just affect children's communication – the ability to understand and be understood – and the development of literacy. It affects their capacity to learn and to think for themselves, their social and emotional development, and their ability to plan, organize, negotiate, compromise and empathize. Yet spoken language gets taken for granted, in government policy, schools, teacher training, and in the curriculum. This we can no longer afford to do. We can no longer assume that children will come into school equipped with all the spoken language they need.

Nor can we ignore the great deal of further learning that needs to go on at school, not just as children mature, but also as part of their educational progress. Ask children to talk in pairs behind a screen, one pair aged 4 or 5 and another aged 10 or 11. It will be immediately obvious which pair is which, but we would probably find it difficult to say exactly how they differ, exactly what it is that the older pair have learned in the intervening six years. We take this development too for granted, assuming it will just happen without direct intervention.

Spoken language needs to be moved to centre-stage, as the most important skill that children need to learn and that teachers need to teach, especially but not only, in the early years. Schools and nurseries are increasingly aware of this, but at the moment they hardly know where to begin. For most of us, spoken language is like a home computer. We have one and we know how to use it. But we don't really understand how it works, and when it isn't working we have little idea what to do about it. For that we need an expert. That's how it has also been with teachers and spoken language. If they became aware of a problem they were expected to seek advice and guidance, from a speech and language therapist or an educational psychologist.

For some children with special educational needs that may still be the case but, increasingly, schools are expected to deal with special needs in the classroom. Moreover, the number of children with inadequate spoken language is now so great that, in most cases, individual advice and support can no longer be expected or made available. It has become a problem that staff have to deal with by themselves, without much in the way of guidance or training. With the best will in the world their intervention may be inappropriate because they do not recognize what is needed or appreciate how very delayed some children's language is, what the educational impact might be, or what can be done about it. This is because they are not trained in teaching spoken language.

Teachers are not trained in the importance of spoken language, its development, or its role in learning and literacy. They are not taught the skills that children need to have when they start school, or the skills they need to develop at school. They are not taught to recognize children with inadequate language, assess the extent of their delay, or how to help them. This huge gap in teacher education is not even recognized as a gap. Here, as elsewhere, spoken language gets taken for granted.

Moreover, such curriculum guidance as exists is inadequate and inappropriate. It assumes too high a level of basic competence and provides insufficient differentiation to help children whose spoken language is impoverished or delayed. The *Early Learning Goals* (QCA, 1999) for children aged 3 to 5, for example, are vague and global, lacking in progression, and do scant justice to the range and complexity of spoken language skills that children actually need in the Foundation Stage. *Speaking, Listening, Learning* (DfES, 2003) for children aged 5 to 11, by contrast, is complex and over-detailed to the point of being almost unmanageable, and largely ignores the link between oracy and literacy, or even – despite its title – between oracy and learning. Ofsted (2005) reports that 'it is rare to find that pupils have targets for speaking and listening, although there are many for whom this is the main obstacle to achievement'. But this is hardly surprising when the targets on offer are so complex and cumbersome.

What our schools need, urgently, is something to bridge this gap between the current lack of training and expertise and the immediate needs of increasing numbers of children. Faced with children who can hardly speak or make themselves understood, who can barely form a coherent sentence or maintain a conversation, who seem not to listen or understand and cannot describe a simple sequence of events, much less explain or predict them, early years staff can be at a loss to know what to do or where to begin. What, exactly, are they supposed to teach these children? How, exactly, do they teach it? And how do they fit that in – whatever it is – on top of everything else they need to be doing?

There are three things that schools and nurseries need to know: what to teach, how to teach it, and how to implement it in the classroom. Each of them introduces a problem: the size and complexity of the spoken language system; the intensity of natural language learning; and the manageability of spoken language teaching. These issues will be addressed in the next three chapters. Their solution lies in being selective in what we teach, systematic in how we teach it, and finding a structured approach that makes spoken language teaching practicable for today's staff in today's classrooms.

A model for teaching spoken language

The first problem for the teaching of spoken language is the sheer amount and complexity of the language that children have to learn. The size of the average vocabulary is astonishing, and so too is the speed and ease with which children usually acquire it. Children entering nursery at the age of 3 can be expected to know 500–1,000 separate words; by the age of 5 they should know 3–5,000; by 10 the figure has risen to 8–10,000 and by 20, at least 20,000. According to one authority (Pinker, 1994) our spoken vocabulary can reach as many as 60,000 words; according to another (Crystal, 1986) we may understand as many as 100,000. And this is only scratching the surface – the *Oxford English Dictionary* currently has 640,000 words and its editors estimate that the revised edition will be twice the size, with 1.3 to 1.6 million items.

Children do not only have to learn vocabulary; they also have to learn a variety of sentence constructions, involving a range of different types of word. They have to learn to put this language to all sorts of different uses, inside and outside school, and they need to develop fluency in all these skills. It is not enough to know the words and grammar and how to use them, especially when it comes to skills like reading and writing. They also have to be able to do it all effortlessly and spontaneously, without needing to think about it.

There is, therefore, much to learn, most of it in the school years. Most children learn from conversation, from teaching, and from reading. Just as spoken language is necessary for literacy, so literacy fuels a huge increase during the primary years both in vocabulary and in more complex sentence constructions. But when this doesn't happen, or when children enter school without the spoken language skills they need, teachers may not know what to do about it. There are so many things the children need to learn, and teachers may have so little training in how to teach it, that it is not surprising if they feel they do not know where to begin.

If we are to cope with all this complexity we need a simple picture or a model of what spoken language is and how it works. Other disciplines – linguistics, psychology, sociology, speech and language therapy – have their own distinctive ways of analysing spoken language but education needs an educational model, one that can structure and guide intervention. It may seem that this needs to be a developmental model. But the development of spoken language is complex, not fully understood and unfamiliar to teachers. Children can vary greatly in their pattern of development or the rate at which they progress, especially in the early years. There is also a great deal going on at any one time. Children do not learn spoken language skills singly or in sequence, they learn bits of everything together. Schools could not easily follow the course of natural development, even if we fully understood it.

What we need instead is a curriculum model, one that identifies the key spoken language skills that children need for progress through school, and introduces them not in the order that they might normally acquire them but in the order they are needed for learning. Many children will acquire these skills in their own way and in their own time, but it is when they are required for the curriculum that staff need to ensure that all children in their class do actually have them. This will also enable language teaching to grow naturally out of other teaching, through the curriculum and teachers' current practice.

The curriculum currently identifies two spoken language skills: speaking and listening. This is an important distinction. Children need to be able to express not merely what they know but also their thoughts and feelings; and they need to be able to listen, to take in what is said to them. But it is not the only distinction, or even the most important, and it is certainly not the place to begin. The model on the opposite page provides the basis for a more detailed and more structured curriculum for spoken language.

The model starts with a distinction between *content* and *use*, between the language we have and what we do with it. Learning spoken language is like learning to drive a car. When we learn to drive we have to learn the mechanics of starting and stopping, slowing down, changing direction and changing gear. But we also have to learn how to use the car on the road: we have to learn when to slow down or speed up, how to pull out into traffic or negotiate a roundabout, and how to take account of other road-users, pedestrians and cyclists as well as drivers. Normally we learn these things together: as we become more adept in the basic skills of manoeuvring the car we also become more adept in using the car on the road. It is the same with spoken language. We have to have the vocabulary and sentence structure that gives content to our language, but we also have to know how to use that content to communicate with other people, in different contexts and for different purposes. These things develop together. Right from the beginning, young children learn to use whatever limited content they have to express their needs, wants and interests to other people.

Content

The content of spoken language consists of words or vocabulary, which are the basic building blocks from which we construct our thoughts, utterances and sentences, and structure or grammar, which is the cement that binds words together and can create different sentences from out of the same ingredients. Clearly, both are needed when children enter school, yet many children lack these elementary skills, or come into nursery at an age when they are still acquiring them.

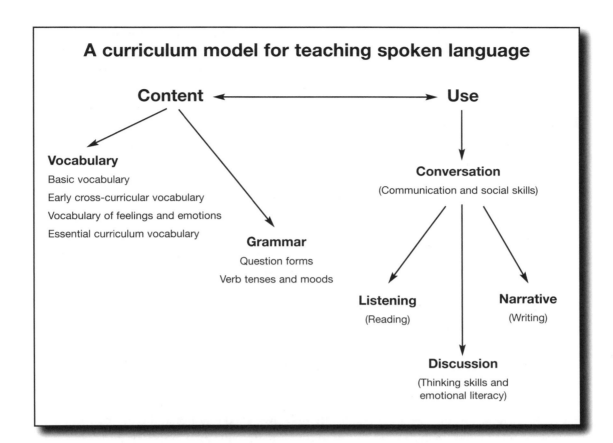

A curriculum model for teaching spoken language

Content ⟷ **Use**

Vocabulary
Basic vocabulary
Early cross-curricular vocabulary
Vocabulary of feelings and emotions
Essential curriculum vocabulary

Grammar
Question forms
Verb tenses and moods

Conversation
(Communication and social skills)

Listening
(Reading)

Narrative
(Writing)

Discussion
(Thinking skills and
emotional literacy)

Vocabulary

Vocabulary is obviously essential for language and communication, and for teaching and learning. Without vocabulary we would have no language at all. We have to use words to teach. The more words that children understand, the more they will learn from others; the more words they can use for themselves, the more they will express, reinforce and extend their learning. Vocabulary is crucial not just for literacy – to understand what we read and know what to write – but for all the curriculum. We need an ever-widening vocabulary both to understand new subjects and topics and to think about them more deeply. These points are discussed in more detail in Chapter 7.

Vocabulary is also a useful indicator of children's cognitive development and their likely progress in school but, except at the earliest stages, we cannot realistically expect to assess the size of children's vocabulary, or use it as a basis for intervention. As we have seen, the number of words that children need to know when they enter school runs into thousands; by the time they leave school, it will be tens of thousands. Schools cannot hope to teach or monitor this number of words systematically.

The curriculum model identifies four types of vocabulary as particularly important.

Basic vocabulary

Most children have developed a vocabulary of several hundred words before they enter nursery and are putting them together to form simple sentences of two or more words. Children who lack this basic vocabulary obviously need to develop it first, not just to understand and be understood but also to help them to develop simple sentence structures. Most children are beginning to produce two-word utterances like *big ball* and *more drink* by the time they know about 20 to 30 different words, and more complex grammar develops spontaneously as they acquire a wider range of different types of word. Children who are not developing simple sentences may need to learn a larger number of words, or be taught different types of word – adjectives, prepositions and adverbs as well as nouns and verbs – before they will start combining them for themselves.

Early cross-curricular vocabulary

There are a large number of words that children need to know for learning in school and for developing more complex and more sophisticated sentences but which they may find difficult because they are more abstract or general than they are used to. These include adjectives of size, shape and colour, prepositions of place and movement, and adverbs like *again* or *always*. These words are particularly important for early maths and science but are essentially cross-curricular and most easily taught and learned through practical activities like art and design, music and PE. Some seem so simple and basic that they are easily taken for granted, but many children need to be taught them explicitly.

The vocabulary of feelings and emotion

Poor behaviour, like poor spoken language, is an increasing problem in today's schools. The two may even be connected. Some unacceptable behaviour may be due to disorders or difficulties; some may be the result of poor management at home or at school; but some of it seems to be sheer inarticulate frustration. Children often lash out or resort to screaming or swearing because they lack the language to direct or control their environment, or express or explain what they are feeling. What is now called emotional literacy or emotional intelligence includes the ability to understand your own emotions and communicate them appropriately, and to recognize and respond appropriately to the feelings of others. This in turn requires the vocabulary to identify and discuss a variety of different feelings and emotions, both positive and negative. This too is something that children may need to be taught.

Essential curriculum vocabulary

Every subject and topic will have its key words that children need to be able to understand and use if they are to learn and talk, or read and write, about it. These are words we may need to teach; they are, in fact, words we have been teaching all along, but perhaps without fully realizing it. Some of them will be new: teaching a new topic is, to a considerable extent, teaching new vocabulary. Others should be familiar, but it cannot be taken for granted that all children in the class will understand them, or be confident in using them. Most subject or topic teaching consists in teaching new words or a fuller understanding of old ones, but this is seldom recognized or made explicit.

Grammar

Vocabulary is vast, grammar is complex. Grammar (meaning by that not capital letters and full stops, or the right mood for a verb in a subordinate clause, but the different ways in which words can be combined together to form sentences) is a difficult technical matter requiring expert analysis. Yet, mysteriously, most adults can use complex grammatical constructions effortlessly and intelligibly, if not always flawlessly. The development of this sentence structure is as important for children's learning and educational progress as is the growth in their vocabulary. They need it for reading and writing, and to grasp and express increasingly sophisticated and complex ideas. Thinking skills, in particular, depend on children's ability to understand and use structures like what *will happen if …* or *what might happen because …*

Children have much to learn here too, mostly in the school years. As with vocabulary, the essentials are laid down early, with greater sophistication coming through the development of literacy. But whereas with vocabulary it may seem easy enough to identify what children know or don't know and what they need to learn, with grammar it is much more difficult for the non-expert to identify what children know or need to be taught, much less know how to teach it. It seems, moreover, difficult if not impossible to teach grammatical forms directly. The most important factors in the development of grammar seem to be the number and range of words that children know, and exposure to model sentences used by adults at a level they can understand and respond to. The more words that children know, and especially the more different types of word they know – not just nouns, verbs and adjectives but prepositions, adverbs and connectives like *if* and *because* – the more likely they are to develop more complex grammatical forms.

The curriculum model provided by *One Step at a Time* identifies two aspects of grammar as particularly important for progress in school.

Question forms

Obviously, school children need to be able to understand questions but they should also be able to ask them. Teachers ask questions all the time and give children lots of practice in answering. They give much less practice, if they give them any, in asking questions. Yet being able to ask a question is every bit as important as being able to answer one. Answering shows what the child does or does not know but asking a question is a way of finding something out, of acquiring new knowledge. It is also a way of demonstrating understanding: a child who asks the right question shows that he has understood. When we don't understand something we don't even know what questions to ask – an experience many of us have had when faced with some bit of new technology.

Question forms are of two main types: verb questions and *wh-* questions. Verb questions change the word order to make a question out of a statement and require a simple yes/no answer, for example 'It will rain' becomes 'Will it rain?' and 'They are coming' becomes 'Are they coming?' *Wh-* questions add an interrogative word such as *what, where, when, why* or *who* (and *how*) to an inverted sentence and require a more detailed or extensive answer. For example, 'Why is he crying?' and 'Where are you going?' Children need to know both forms, both in asking questions and in answering them.

Verb tenses and moods

Children have to understand tenses in order to understand stories and other narratives, and they have to be able to use them to write coherent texts themselves. But an understanding of tenses also gives them an understanding of time itself, and the difference between present, past and future. This is crucial not only for a subject like history but also in science, where children have to predict what *will* happen or explain what *did* happen. Similarly, modal verbs like *could, might* or *should* are needed to understand possibility and probability as well as actuality, and therefore essential not just for science but for any activity that involves anticipation, prediction or planning.

Use

Language is a tool. To get the most out of it you have to know how to use it, and the more you can use it the more you can get from it. As well as learning the words and constructions that make up spoken language, children have to learn how to use them to express their needs and wants, to ask questions, to make requests to give instructions and for many other functions.

We have become familiar with the idea of different uses of written language: descriptions, reports, imaginative stories, factual accounts, personal letters, formal applications. It is less often noticed that talk has different uses too. We use spoken language to ask, instruct and entertain; to make friends and influence people; to approve, apologize and argue. Each of these may have a different 'voice' or 'register': there are rules and customs about how to talk for different purposes, with different people and in different contexts. Children have to learn not only not to talk in class in the way that they would talk at home, but also not, to speak to an adult in the way that they might speak to their friends. They also need to learn how to listen, to join a discussion, to ask a question or make a suggestion. Children who lack these skills may be ostracized or bullied, can be difficult in class and unpopular with staff as well as with other children.

Vocabulary is vast, grammar is complex, use is elusive. The uses of spoken language and the skills they involve are difficult to classify. As with vocabulary and grammar, it is hard to know where to begin. Here, too, we need to identify the skills that children are going to need for learning in school.

In the curriculum model the key skills are conversation, listening, narrative and discussion. Each of these is complex and demanding. They combine and overlap, and become relevant at different times and during different activities. They develop together but we cannot teach them all at once. Instead, we have to separate them and teach them in the order that is most relevant and useful in the classroom.

Conversation comes first because it is the most basic, for communication, for teaching and learning, and for social development. Listening is equally crucial for understanding and learning, and especially the development of reading. Narrative or extended talk is important for developing coherent thinking and the expression of ideas, and therefore for writing. Discussion, finally, is an under-recognized but no less crucial element in the development of cross-curricular thinking skills. These include the ability to formulate and reflect on ideas; to consider hypotheses and make predictions; to plan, agree and compromise; and to understand other people's thoughts, feelings and behaviour. This sequence of skills makes sense in both curriculum and developmental terms. Conversation feeds into and develops extended listening and extended speaking, and they all feed into discussion, which is a form of extended conversation.

Conversation

Conversation is the most basic form of spoken communication and an essential social skill. It is through conversation that we learn to speak in the first place. Conversation is also the means by which adults develop children's spoken language and provide them with a model of how language works. It underpins other learning and is the basis of most classroom teaching, especially but not only, in the early years. Children need conversation not only to communicate with others but also to learn about the world, to express their thoughts and feelings and to make friendships. These points are discussed in more detail in Chapter 10.

Listening

Listening is a crucial classroom skill, for literacy and for other learning. Children have to be able to attend, concentrate and remember, follow directions and instructions, and grasp and retain information. They have to be able to discriminate the sounds in words in order to read, write and spell. They have to be able to follow stories and other narratives, and understand implicit or contextual meanings. Moreover, the type of extended listening expected in school is more complex and demanding than the conversational listening most children are used to. They have to be able to attend and concentrate in larger groups, over longer periods and in a larger space, without being able to reply or respond until they are told to. These points are discussed in more detail in Chapter 11.

Narrative

Narrative is connected or extended talk, as in describing something in detail, recalling an event, retelling a story, or talking about what you plan to do. It requires children to put thoughts and sentences together in a more systematic and structured way than in simple conversation. As they progress through school they need to develop this more formal type of talking in order to report events or activities, to explain how something was made, or to predict the outcomes of experiments. This develops their thinking skills and is essential for formal writing. To write even a simple account they have to be able to think of something to write about, put it in the right order, mention the key facts and exclude irrelevant detail, and to provide a beginning and an ending. They will not be able to do this in their writing unless they are first able to do it in their talk. These points are discussed in more detail in Chapter 12.

Discussion

Discussion is a form of extended conversation, where children talk together about what they have learned, how to find something out, how to plan an activity or how to solve a problem. This requires both extended listening and extended speaking, develops children's confidence, social skills and thinking skills, and encourages co-operation and active learning, with children working together to find things out for themselves. Discussion can also be used to negotiate and resolve problems and differences, and develop emotional literacy. It is a powerful teaching and learning tool with older children. These points are discussed in more detail in Chapter 13.

Fluency

All this takes time. Even when children grow up in ideal conditions it takes several years to establish a basic vocabulary, basic grammar and basic competence in language use – and these skills continue to develop and consolidate through the primary years and into secondary school. But children also need to develop fluency in all these skills. We can, once again, compare acquiring spoken language with learning to drive a car. It is not enough that we know how to brake or change gear, turn a corner or overtake. To be a good driver who is safe to be let out on the road we have to be able to do these things effortlessly and spontaneously, without having to think about them, so we can concentrate instead on where we are going, what the other traffic is doing, or what other hazards there might be – let alone talking to a passenger or listening to the radio.

Similarly with spoken language. Children need fluency in spoken language to free up capacity for learning and thinking, and for reading and writing. Teachers are familiar with children at all ages, right through to secondary school, who seem to have mastered the mechanics of reading in that they can read text off the page, yet seem to make little sense of what they are reading. This is because, if they find reading at all difficult, they have to put so much effort into decoding the written marks that they have no capacity left to take in the meaning. It is only if they are already so thoroughly familiar with the spoken form of the language that they can grasp the meaning effortlessly and spontaneously, without having to think about it, that they will be able to understand at the same time as they read.

It is the same with thinking skills. If children have to concentrate on understanding the words we are using, they will not at the same time be able to think about what we are saying. If they have to work hard to find the words to express themselves they will not at the same time be able to think about what they are trying to say. Children who lack experience or confidence in talking to adults or other children or have never learned to listen properly to what others are saying to them, may have such difficulty in knowing what to say or how to respond that they are unable to reflect on what they need to know or find out, much less explore ideas or initiate questions themselves.

If children are to use language in thinking and learning they need to be so familiar with it, and so fluent in it, that the words go in through their ears, into their minds and out through their mouths, effortlessly, automatically, spontaneously. Everyone needs practice and experience to develop confidence and fluency in the use of a new skill, and some children will need longer than others.

3

Learning and teaching spoken language

The last chapter looked at the difficulties posed by the complexity of spoken language. The second problem for the teaching of spoken language is the intensity of natural language learning. Most children acquire spoken language so quickly and so easily that it almost seems spontaneous, but it is not as spontaneous as it appears. We fail to notice the huge exposure to spoken language that most children receive. Talk is part of their natural environment. They are surrounded by it, not just by talk but by talk to them and about them, about what they are wearing, what they are doing, what it is they want to do.

Learning language at home

Parents talk to their children almost from birth, and even before. Right from the beginning they attempt to engage their babies in mock conversations, in language they seem to expect the baby to understand. And, astonishingly, the baby seems to respond, almost as soon as he is able to do anything. These responses – every smile, every noise, every sound, and eventually every word – are rewarded with smiles, encouragement and more talk. Then when the child responds, first with noises, then with baby sounds, and finally with attempted words, the adult interprets what the child is 'saying', giving it a meaning and introducing the relevant language: 'Oh, you want a drink, do you? Yes, you can have a drink.' When the child starts to talk the adult adjusts her own talk to a level she thinks the child will understand, but amplifies or explains what he is trying to say and adds the words she thinks he needs or will find useful: 'Mummy shop!' 'Yes, mummy's gone to the shop to buy some milk. She'll be back soon.'

The key factors in this process seem to be:

◆ *Adult–child interaction*: Most talk to babies or toddlers is adult to child, one-to-one. The adult gives the child her undivided attention. She takes her cue from him. She can see what the child is doing, and what interests or engages him. She talks about it in a way she expects him to understand, and uses his response as a basis for her own.

◆ *Familiar activities*: Adult and child play together or share familiar routines like dressing or feeding. The child is actively involved, doing real things with real objects (including toys), not sitting passively looking at pictures or listening to stories. The adult talks about what the child is doing. This physical activity with physical things gives the words meaning for him. Familiar activities with familiar objects in familiar situations mean that the child already knows what the words are about – what they mean – before he learns the words themselves. He only has to learn one thing, not two.

◆ *Active encouragement*: Children are encouraged to talk, and talk is expected of them – parents positively demand a response even from young babies. Children learn to talk in the best way for anyone to learn anything, actively not passively, by doing it for themselves. They learn to talk by talking.

◆ *Repetition, repetition, repetition*: All this happens again and again, the same words and the same phrases, day after day, week after week. With very young children, adults seem to feel a compulsion to say everything twice. Older children like to hear the same songs and stories over and over again, and they like to repeat the same words and phrases themselves, during the same routines, day after day. Children don't just learn language; they over-learn it.

It may be the inadequacy of this experience for some children that, more than anything else, accounts for the growing numbers entering schools and nurseries with limited spoken language. Detailed observation of 42 American families (Hart and Risley, 1995) showed striking differences in the amount that parents talked to their one- and two-year-old children. The differences seemed to be cultural and strongly associated with socio-economic status. On average, professional parents talked to their children more than three times as much as parents on welfare; 'blue collar' parents twice as much. As a result it would have taken the children from the welfare group another seven years to get the same exposure to parental language as the children of professional parents had already received by the age of three. By the age of three children from the professional group already had a bigger vocabulary than the parents on welfare!

There were differences in quality as well as quantity. The professional parents used more types of word, more multi-clause sentences, more past and future tenses, and more questions of all kinds. They also gave their children more affirmative feedback and responded to them more often. The professional parents gave their children six times as many affirmations, and half as many prohibitions; and because of the difference in the total amount of talk, while about 80 per cent of the professional parents' feedback to their children was positive, about 80 per cent of the welfare parents' feedback was negative.

> *The accomplishments of the higher-SES children are hardly surprising when we consider their cumulative experience: three years of enriched language and activities; three years of being told they were 'right' and 'good'; and three years of frequently being chosen as more interesting to listen to and talk to than anyone else.*

Betty Hart & Todd R. Risley (1995) *Meaningful Differences in the Everyday Experience of Young American Children*, page 183, Paul H. Brookes Publishing Company, Baltimore, reprinted by permission

Learning language at school

Early years interventions from Head Start in the USA to SureStart in England and Wales have tried to compensate for disadvantages such as these, but it is hardly surprising that they have met with only limited success. In the American research it would have taken an additional 41 hours a week to give children from the welfare families the same exposure to spoken language as the children from 'blue collar' homes; to give them the same exposure as the professional children would have taken 102 hours. Intervention on that scale is far beyond the resources of almost any compensatory programme.

It is, moreover, hard to imagine a worse environment for learning spoken language than the typical classroom.

◆ *Adult–child interaction*: This is recognized as important with nursery children but is more difficult to provide in later years. Even in nurseries a ratio of 1 adult to 8 children is viewed as an ideal; more often it is 1 to 12 or 13. Staff in schools cannot possibly give every child undivided personal attention. There are not enough people in the room, not enough time in the day, too much pressure to do too many other things. Children have to be taught in groups, large or small, most of the time. It has been calculated that each primary school child gets, on average, just two minutes of personal interaction with their teacher each day. Adults cannot tune into the talk of individual children and respond at the level that is appropriate for each of them. Personal feedback is limited, often non-existent, sometimes negative.

◆ *Familiar activities*: Adult talk does not necessarily relate to what children are currently doing or are interested in. The activities children engage in and the language to be used are largely imposed on the child, driven by the daily timetable and the demands of the curriculum. Schools provide new and unfamiliar experiences, not just at first with their new surroundings and unfamiliar adults and children, but because their whole purpose is to introduce children to new ideas, new activities, new materials. Children have to learn new language at the same time as they learn new things. That makes it twice as difficult.

◆ *Active encouragement*: Too often, spontaneous talk is not encouraged or positively discouraged, no matter how interesting or urgent the topic may be: 'Sit quietly now and listen.' Most school talk is teacher talk. Teachers talk much of the time and children listen, or speak only when spoken to. Too often, a good classroom is still supposed to be a quiet classroom.

◆ *Repetition, repetition, repetition*: Constant repetition and over-learning are a luxury most schools feel they cannot afford. Many children are not given sufficient time to consolidate new skills or develop fluency. There is too much pressure to move everyone on as quickly as possible.

When the conditions are right, and at the right age, language learning can be effortless, natural and apparently automatic. But those conditions cannot easily be created in schools or nurseries. We need to reproduce them where we can, and compensate for them where we cannot.

◆ *Adult–child interaction*: Staff spend a lot of time talking to children – instructing, questioning, explaining – but this is not the same as talking with them, listening to them and responding at a level that interests and engages them. The key to this is conversation. Conversation is not just a basic skill that children need to learn; it is also the means by which we teach and learn spoken language, and many other skills as well. Conversation enables staff to monitor children's understanding and to ensure that what they are saying themselves is at the right level. They need to be sensitive to the language that children are actually using so they can build on it. They also need to be sensitive to their own language to ensure it is at the right level for children to understand and use for themselves. If these are badly out of balance, much of what staff say will pass the children by.

All staff should maximize the opportunities for personal conversation, making the best use of those that are available and creating new opportunities wherever they can. There are many idle moments in the day, when children are coming into class or waiting in line, snack-time and playtime, when staff can engage them in one-to-one conversation. Free activity sessions and playtimes can also provide good opportunities for promoting talk between children as well as with adults. Everyone – not just teachers but all staff – has a role to play in making time to talk with individual children. Every child should have at least one extended conversation with an adult every day. Parents can help too, by being encouraged to chat over the day's activities with their children.

◆ *Familiar activities*: The familiar daily routines of eating and drinking, washing and toileting, dressing and undressing, provide much the best starting points for teaching language to young children. Older children, too, will learn new language more quickly if they can be involved in an activity that brings a topic to life, rather than just sitting listening to someone talking about it. Even simple activities like cutting out and pasting pictures seem to support language learning more than talk on its own.

Choice of activities and materials is also important: they should be interesting and enjoyable but not too demanding. The contexts, materials and activities need to be thoroughly familiar. If they are unfamiliar children are being expected to learn several things at once – not just the new word or expression but what it means, and possibly also the activity being used to teach it. Where an activity or materials are unfamiliar, children should be allowed to become familiar with them before being expected to learn new skills. Similarly, it is always best to start a language-teaching session with familiar activities, especially before introducing a new item, and to repeat activities for at least a week so that children can become familiar with them.

◆ *Active encouragement*: What is needed most of all is a change of focus, from teachers' talk to children's talk. Children need to be encouraged to talk, whenever and wherever possible. They should be encouraged to say what they want to say, about what interests them. They should be made to feel that their talk will be valued and listened to, that if they attempt to say something they will be supported, not silenced.

This includes children talking to each other. A quiet classroom is *not* a good classroom. The buzz of a busy – not a noisy – classroom is the sign of a classroom where talk is valued. Adults find it easiest to chat over food or a drink, and deliberately set this up when they want to 'catch up' with friends. Yet there are still schools where children are forbidden to talk during meal-times. Free activity sessions are another good indicator: do children talk to each other as they play, or do they play silently on their own?

Of course, children cannot talk all the time. There may have to be rules, discussed with and explained to them, about when they can talk or where they can talk. There may need to be 'talk-spaces' and 'talk-times'. But in general and wherever possible, children's talk should be encouraged, not discouraged.

◆ *Repetition, repetition, repetition*: Staff sometimes think they need to keep changing stories or activities to retain children's interest and broaden their experience. But as every parent knows, young children love to repeat the same things over and over again: the same story, the same song, the same little phrases, the same little routines, day after day. Children need this constant repetition to acquire, consolidate and generalize language and develop fluency.

The same level of repetition needs to be reproduced in school. Stories, songs and nursery rhymes may need to be repeated for days, even weeks, before children really understand them or know the words. Teaching activities and the language that goes with them, similarly, may need to be repeated many times, possibly for several weeks with younger children. This takes patience, even courage, in today's climate, where the pressure is to move everyone on as quickly as possible. But it needs to be done, especially if children are having difficulty.

For any of this to happen, everyone in the school needs to recognize that talk matters, that talk is the place to start, and that children who cannot talk and listen properly will not progress at school. It should be part of everyone's job description – not just teachers and classroom staff but playground supervisors, dinner ladies and site staff – that they talk with children whenever and wherever possible. It should be part of every school activity – daily routines, lessons, outings and visits – that adults talk with children about it, individually and together, before it has begun, while it is happening, and when it is finished. And, of course, this means not talking *at* them or to them but *with* them.

Children's talk also needs to be recognized, more than it is, as a way of learning. Children, like adults, learn more and more quickly if they can be active not passive, if they can be in control of their learning. They can learn, not only from teachers' talk but also from their own talk, as much as from listening, reading or writing. At all ages and in all subjects, right through to secondary school, there should be less reliance on initiation and response teaching – question and answer, listen then do – or solitary reading and writing, and more emphasis on talking as a way of learning. For example:

◆ *Do* and *Review* where children consolidate and reinforce their learning by discussing together what they have just done or learned, or *Plan*, *Do* and *Review* where they discuss what they are going to do or what they need to learn or find out (see Chapters 7 and 8 of the Activities Handbook in *Teaching Talking*, Locke and Beech, 2005).

◆ New topics can be introduced by getting children to discuss what they already know about it, and what they need to learn or find out. This not only shares existing knowledge across the class and helps the teacher focus her teaching where it is most needed, it also helps children to learn and use the new language for themselves.

- ◆ Each child can have a talking partner, so they can consolidate and reinforce their learning by talking it over in pairs (see Chapter 12).

- ◆ Older children can learn actively by discussing a topic with other children, with or without adult supervision (see Chapter 13).

Teaching spoken language systematically

All this will help, but it will not be enough on its own. The conditions that promote natural language learning are only part of the story. There is more to learning spoken language than being exposed, in the right conditions, to good adult models. Children are not simply surrounded by spoken language, immersed in it like a baby in bathwater. We actually teach children how to talk, and how to listen, without quite realizing we are doing it. The techniques by which we do this will be discussed in Chapter 6, but in schools we have to use them explicitly and systematically, knowing exactly what we are doing.

There is in fact – there has to be – one essential difference between natural language learning and language teaching at school. Natural language learning is spontaneous, informal and child-led. Adults use every opportunity to encourage children's talk without any very firm idea of what they are teaching or what children need to learn. There is no plan or strategy that they are working to. They simply pick up on what the children are doing and saying, and follow that. But the interaction is so intensive and extensive – hour after hour, day after day, month after month, year after year – that children absorb an enormous amount, almost without our noticing it.

Schools and nurseries cannot possibly work like that. Language learning cannot be allowed to just happen, as it does at home. In schools and nurseries, language teaching has to be organized, systematic and staff-led. Staff have to decide what to teach, how to teach it and when to teach it. They have to focus on specific items; they have to teach them explicitly and systematically, to all children; and they have to ensure that all children do learn them. Lessons have to be planned, prepared and timetabled; individual progress has to be assessed and monitored. None of this will happen at home, but it has to happen at school. This is how we teach a second, or a third, language at school. It should be how we teach a first language too.

If teaching is focused and systematic, moreover, children should be able to learn more, hour for hour, than they would learn from informal exposure and encouragement. This is the difference between picking up a skill from observing and copying an experienced practitioner and being taught it explicitly and systematically. What language teaching in school lacks in quantity, in the sheer amount of exposure and adult–child interaction, it will have to make up in quality, focus and rigour, efficiency and effectiveness.

Which brings us to the third main issue for the teaching of spoken language in schools and nurseries: its manageability.

Managing language teaching in the classroom

There is a huge amount of spoken language that children need to learn, even if staff are selective in what they teach and reduce it to the essential vocabulary and skills needed for progress at school. There is also a great deal that staff need to do to ensure that all children acquire these skills. They need to provide an environment that promotes language learning; they need to provide appropriate contexts and stimulation; they need to teach specific items and skills systematically and explicitly; they need to give the practice and repetition that will enable all children to achieve fluency; and they need to monitor individual progress and the effectiveness of their own teaching methods.

This may be starting to seem impossibly demanding. A spoken language syllabus will have to be developed and agreed. Lessons will have to be planned, prepared and timetabled. Individual children will have to be assessed and monitored. Room for all of this will have to be found within an already overcrowded timetable and a curriculum that is already overburdened with too many other initiatives. Schools have limited time, staff and other resources. And on top of all that, teachers generally don't have training and expertise in teaching spoken language, and such curriculum guidance as exists is inadequate and often inappropriate.

It need not, however, be as demanding as it seems. First, spoken language should not be thought of as yet another subject that teachers need to teach and children need to learn. It is, rather, a set of skills that teachers need to use if they are going to teach anything, and that children need to use if they are going to learn anything. Used properly, spoken language teaching should not increase the burden; it should reduce it, by making other teaching and learning simpler and more accessible.

These are, moreover, cross-curricular skills, and skills that can be used with any curriculum content. They are needed for every subject and can be taught in any subject. Much of what we need is there already, in the existing timetable and curriculum, provided we make the crucial shift of focus from teachers' talk to children's talk. Staff may need to designate specific times of the day for teaching specific items and skills, but this should not mean fitting yet more things into an already overcrowded timetable. Spoken language should be taught in the context of familiar activities, including informal activities and daily routines. Language teaching should make use of activities that are already going on every day, and build language work around them.

Schools should also make use of the adults that are available already, not just school staff but parents, grandparents, other volunteers and even visitors. Another underutilized resource is the children themselves. In most schools learning is seen as essentially an individual and solitary exercise. Even quite young children are expected to attend to the teacher, then work on their own. Helping one another or copying other children are often seen as inappropriate, unfair or even cheating. Yet through their school years children learn as much from other children – perhaps not always what we want them to learn – as from the staff. Imitation, copying and following the example of others are powerful learning mechanisms. This applies as much to language learning as any other skill, and in working together, no matter what the topic, children will at the same time be developing their spoken language.

Paired and independent group work is particularly valuable for allowing children more time than staff can normally afford for practising and consolidating skills and developing fluency. As with the use of other adults in the classroom – parents and volunteers as well as support staff – it can also be used to free up time to allow teachers to work on specific skills, including language skills, with other children. There may be concern that, left to themselves, children will go off task and become disruptive but, for most children, this is unlikely provided the task is familiar and at an appropriate level.

It may also have the advantage of swimming with the tide. A recent review of inspection evidence (Ofsted, 2005) reports that 'too few lessons now use small group work effectively'. It 'has been a positive development in some schools and provides the teacher with an opportunity to demonstrate different kinds of spoken language as well as supporting pupils' reading and writing work [but] is an underused approach in many schools'. 'Some primary teachers have responded positively and are trying to use pupils' collaborative talk more often through the use of "talk partners", but in most classrooms activities to develop pupils' talk remains limited.' 'Many teachers still need to have the courage to be innovative, making greater use, in particular, of group, collaborative and independent approaches and a wider range of teaching strategies to engage and challenge pupils.'

Structured language teaching

Once again, all this will help, but it will not be enough on its own. Schools and staff will still need something that takes the difficulty out of language teaching, that tells them what to teach, when to teach it, how to teach it and how to assess individual progress. They will need a curriculum, syllabus or teaching programme that:

- ◆ is simple, straightforward and self-explanatory, easy to understand and use;
- ◆ identifies the items and skills they need to teach, in the order in which they need to teach them;
- ◆ describes ways of teaching these items and skills to all children in the class, and ensuring that all children learn them;
- ◆ enables staff to monitor individual progress, assess individual differences and provide teaching that is sufficiently differentiated to meet the needs of all children in the class;

◆ embodies the expertise in teaching spoken language that teachers currently lack, and helps them to acquire it for themselves from practical experience.

To achieve this we first need to take the various skills identified in the model of spoken language in Chapter 2 and break them down into their component sub-skills. Conversation or listening, for example, are not single skills. They consist of a number of subordinate skills such as knowing how to initiate a conversation or being able to discriminate sounds in words. Each of these divides in turn into further sub-skills, such as greeting someone, looking at them or showing interest in what they say, or being able to recognize the initial sound of a word or identify rhymes. With other complex skills like literacy or numeracy we are familiar with the idea that we need to break them down into component skills and teach them one by one over a period of weeks or even years. It is the same with spoken language.

This will also ensure that staff focus on specific skills and items for teaching to all children in their class. If teaching objectives are too global, as with the *Early Learning Goals* (QCA, 1999), staff will be trying to teach too much at once. Intervention will become unfocused and learning will be difficult to monitor. Precise objectives make it clear what staff need to teach, what children need to learn and what behaviours they need to demonstrate. They also help staff to identify children's current skills and discriminate their different levels of development.

These skills and sub-skills then need to be put in a sequence or progression, based on the order in which children need to learn them. This will allow teaching to build skill upon skill, week after week, term after term, year after year, through the crucial period when most children are establishing the basic components of spoken language (ages 3 to 5), and beginning to develop fluency and variety (ages 5 to 6), up to at least the end of Key Stage 1 (ages 6 to 7). This step-by-step approach will tell staff exactly what to teach and when, enable them to plan lessons in advance, prepare suitable activities and materials, advise support staff and inform parents.

This structured approach to language teaching has another important advantage. By making explicit the structure of skills that children need to learn if they are to progress in school, it will make staff more aware of the importance of spoken language, more knowledgeable about its development, and more observant of children's current abilities and the impact on their other learning. It will, in short, embody the expertise that teachers need, and help them to learn for themselves from experience, discussion and collaboration with their colleagues. It will build their confidence in teaching spoken language at the same time as it builds children's competence in using spoken language.

There is, however, one further essential requirement. A spoken language curriculum, syllabus or programme needs to be easy to implement and manage in the classroom. It must be something that schools and staff can manage on existing resources, with current expertise, and within the current timetable. It must:

◆ build on existing classroom activities and the current curriculum;

◆ require a minimum of additional training, staffing or other resources;

◆ be adaptable to the differing needs of different schools, different teachers and different children.

This, too, is not impossible. It is precisely what *One Step at a Time* sets out to do.

5

One Step at a Time

One Step at a Time is a structured programme for the systematic teaching of spoken language in nurseries and primary schools from the nursery year (children aged 3 or 4) through to Year 2 (children aged 6 or 7). It can be extended into Key Stage 2 (children aged 7 or 8 and upwards), and its principles and practices continue to apply through primary school and into secondary school.

One Step at a Time is based on the following ideas (see Chapters 1–4):

◆ inadequate spoken language is increasingly recognized as *the* major problem in early years education, inhibiting the development of literacy, social skills, thinking and learning skills, and emotional literacy;

◆ the development of spoken language skills should therefore be the main priority from ages 3 to 5, and a joint priority with literacy from 5 to 7 and beyond;

◆ spoken language skills need to be promoted and monitored in all children, not just those who are identified as having special educational needs or children for whom English is an additional language;

◆ spoken language is a complex system, not fully understood, that needs to be made accessible to teaching staff in a way that reflects and supports the wider school curriculum;

◆ classroom staff need to have specific teaching objectives and simple ways of screening all children and monitoring individual progress;

◆ the programme must be easily manageable within the classroom, without adding appreciably to the workload of teachers or requiring additional resources or special expertise;

◆ it should therefore build on existing classroom practice and activities and be adaptable to the needs of different schools, different teachers and different children.

One Step at a Time aims to make spoken language teaching manageable in the classroom by:

◆ concentrating on the spoken language skills that are most critical for educational progress;

◆ identifying different sorts of skill that can be taught year by year;

◆ breaking these down into sub-skills that can be taught week by week, term by term;

◆ ensuring that these skills are taught one by one to all children in the class or group.

So it's 'One Step at a Time', for staff as well as children. At the same time that children gain confidence and experience by learning one skill at a time, staff will gain confidence and expertise from teaching one skill at a time.

Each year of the programme focuses on a specific set of skills that are crucial for progress at school and beyond (see Chapter 2).

◆ *Conversation* is the most basic form of spoken communication and an essential social skill. It is how we learn to speak in the first place, and the means by which adults develop children's spoken language and provide them with a model of how language works. It underpins other learning and is the basis of most classroom teaching, especially but not only in the early years. Children need conversation, not only to communicate with others, but also to learn about the world, to express their thoughts and feelings and to make friendships.

◆ *Listening* is a crucial classroom skill. Children have to be able to attend, concentrate and remember; follow directions and instructions; understand and retain information; and discriminate sounds in words in order to read, write and spell. They need to be able to follow stories and other narratives, and understand implicit or contextual meanings. Moreover, the extended listening that is expected in school is more complex and demanding than the conversational listening most children are used to. They have to be able to attend and concentrate in larger groups, over longer periods and in a larger space, without being able to reply or respond until they are told to. Children need these skills not just for literacy but for all learning at school.

◆ *Narrative* is connected or extended talk. It requires children to put sentences and thoughts together in a more systematic and structured way than in simple conversation. Children need to develop this more formal type of talking in order to report events or activities, explain how something was made, or predict the outcomes of experiments. Learning to do this is essential for formal writing and also develops children's thinking skills.

◆ *Discussion* is a form of extended conversation, where children talk together about what they have learned, or how to find something out, plan an activity or solve a problem. It requires both extended listening and extended speaking, develops children's confidence, social skills and thinking skills, and encourages both co-operation and active learning. Discussion can also be used to negotiate and resolve problems and differences, and to develop emotional literacy. It is a powerful teaching and learning tool with older children.

In *One Step at a Time* each of these skills is developed over the course of a school year:

◆ *Conversation skills* in the nursery year (children aged 3 or 4);

◆ *Listening skills* in reception (children aged 4 or 5);

◆ *Narrative skills* in Year 1 (children aged 5 or 6);

◆ *Discussion skills* in Year 2 (children aged 6 or 7).

There is also a preliminary step to the programme – *Getting started* – for children who lack basic language skills and are not ready for systematic work on conversation. Some schools and nurseries may want to begin with *Getting started* for all their children before moving on to *Conversation skills*.

At each main step of the programme there is:

◆ an initial screen for assessing children's competence in the relevant skills;

◆ three skills checklists for guiding intervention and reviewing progress over the course of the year;

◆ a vocabulary list of 100 key words for systematic teaching to all children in the class;

◆ information on classroom procedure, advice on teaching methods and detailed notes on each skills checklist.

The content and procedure for *Getting started* is different from the other steps (see Chapter 9).

The vocabulary lists are selected from basic vocabulary, early cross-curricular vocabulary and the vocabulary of feelings and emotions, and are meant to be supplemented with a selection of essential curriculum vocabulary. These are identified in the curriculum model of spoken language (Chapter 2) as being particularly important for children's progress in school. The model also identifies question forms and verb tenses and moods as the most crucial aspects of grammar. These are included under *Listening skills* (understanding question forms), *Narrative skills* (asking questions, verb tenses) and *Discussion skills* (verb moods).

One Step at a Time uses a mixture of whole-class teaching, small-group or paired work, and individual or informal interaction to provide teaching in spoken language skills for all children in the class. The balance changes as children move through the programme from the nursery year (ages 3 or 4) to Year 2 (ages 6 or 7) but the emphasis throughout is on providing opportunities for individual children to speak and listen with an adult and/or a few other children. Whole-class teaching is used to introduce, consolidate and generalize individual learning in group, paired and one-to-one work.

One Step at a Time provides differentiated teaching to meet the needs of all children. It is an 'all needs' programme not a special needs programme: children with identifiable special needs may need additional support (see the section in Chapter 8 on children with special educational needs). Nor is it a programme specifically for children with speech, language or communication disorders. All children in the class will benefit from the extra practice and experience in speaking and listening, but *One Step at a Time* will particularly benefit those children who are sometimes overlooked because they are slower learners without being identified as having a special need.

Ideally, every child in the class will receive personal intervention, and progress and learning will be monitored individually. But realistically this is not always possible and detailed intervention may have to be focused on children who are slower to acquire the relevant skills. *One Step at a Time* uses a simple screen to identify the amount of support needed for each child. The skills checklists, similarly, are used to set teaching objectives for all children on a rolling basis, but can also be used to monitor the learning of selected children.

This concentrated approach should not increase the burden on school and nursery staff. Instead, *One Step at a Time* should take the effort out of language teaching by embodying the expertise that teachers need, telling them what to teach, when and how, and showing how spoken language can relate to the rest of the curriculum. Moreover, *One Step at a Time* will often overlap with other initiatives and programmes – *Listening skills* with phonics programmes, *Discussion skills* with thinking skills programmes, vocabulary work with maths, science and emotional literacy programmes – and can be customized to work with them. Staff who have used the programme have commented that the content is not so very different from what they were doing before but *One Step at a Time* gives them a focus and a method, so they can see more clearly what they need to do and how they need to do it. Their increasing awareness of children's current spoken language and the skills that children need to learn leads them to adjust their practice almost without noticing it. So in the end 'It's just common sense really.'

The key to all this, for both children and staff, is confidence.

◆ Confidence is where *One Step at a Time* begins, with the very first checklist of *Getting started* – and confidence is often all these children need to get started (page 80).

◆ Confidence is the most basic of the 'four Cs' (page 69) – *confidence, curiosity, concentration* and *communication* – which feed into the fifth C, and the first step of the programme proper, *Conversation*.

◆ Confidence is what staff need to look for, in assessing or teaching any skill: that children are using it *confidently, competently* and *consistently* (pages 43 and 49).

◆ Confidence is what staff need to aim for, in themselves, to deliver the programme: they need to be *comfortable* and *confident* in what they are doing if it is to benefit the children they are teaching (page 41).

And time and again, confidence is what staff who have used the programme report: how very much more confident their children are – especially the less able children – in their talking, reading and writing. In their learning and social skills they are more willing to try, more willing to have a go, more engaged in the experiences being offered to them, more able to learn from them.

6

Using the programme

This chapter describes the general procedures for implementing *One Step at a Time* in schools and nurseries. It covers:

◆ initial screening

◆ the skills checklists

◆ classroom intervention

◆ lesson planning

◆ teaching method

◆ reviewing progress and moving on.

Vocabulary teaching is dealt with separately in the next chapter. Detailed procedures and advice for each step in the programme (including *Getting started*) is given in Chapters 9–13. A number of specific issues, including introducing the programme into a school or nursery, training and inducting staff, involving parents, and working with children who develop more slowly than other children in the class, are dealt with in Chapter 8.

The procedures are written as if they are instructions to be followed strictly, but that is only because that is the simplest way to introduce and explain them. They are meant to be interpreted flexibly, in whatever way best suits the school, its staff and its children. It is crucial that staff feel comfortable and confident in what they are doing, and they will only feel that if they can gain ownership of the programme by adapting it to their needs and purposes and fitting it in with other projects and activities. As with reading, there is not one right way to teach children language skills; the right way is whatever way works for staff and children. But, that said, staff may find it easiest to follow the programme strictly at first, and then vary it as they gain in confidence and experience.

Initial screening

Initial screening has two important functions:

◆ to help staff tune into children's current spoken language and the skills to be taught in the current year;

◆ to identify the level of support that needs to be given to each child.

It is important to consider children individually because it is so easy to take these skills for granted. It is, for example, easy to underestimate the skills of quiet or shy children or overestimate the skills of more talkative ones. Staff may also be surprised to discover just how delayed some children actually are: to discover, for example, that in a class of 30 children, only two had any idea how to clap in time to music.

The initial screens are quick and simple measures of current development, not formal assessments. They classify children into three groups, though staff who have used the screens report that they are still very useful even if they do not use them for grouping children, because of the insight they provide into individual children. The groupings are:

◆ *Competent*, that is, children who seem to be acquiring the relevant skills without too much difficulty. These children are not expected to need special attention but staff should keep an eye on them and move them to one of the other categories if they seem to be having any difficulty with the relevant skills;

◆ *Developing*, that is, children who seem to be slower in acquiring the relevant skills. These children may need assistance in acquiring these skills, and will benefit from support and monitoring;

◆ *Delayed*, that is, children who seem to be having difficulty in acquiring the relevant skills and are likely to need more intensive support and monitoring.

This is only an initial classification. Children may be moved from one category to another on the basis of progress during the year. Young children are particularly likely to underperform, because they are shy or nervous or new to the school or nursery.

Initial screening should take place as early in the year as possible, but not until children have settled in and become used to their new environment and staff have been able to form a reasonable impression of their abilities. Where children are new to a particular school or early years setting it may be sensible to wait until the first half-term break, but screening should not be delayed beyond that.

Screening should be carried out by at least two members of staff working together. It may sometimes be useful to involve a member of staff from the previous year but screening needs to focus on children's competence in the skills to be taught in the current year. Children may well be in different categories in different years because they deal with different skills, for example children who are good at conversation may be poor at listening, and vice versa.

Procedure

❖ Once children have settled into their new class staff should spend at least a week observing their spoken language in a variety of situations, both formal and informal, and focusing on the skills that are to be assessed.

❖ They should then complete the initial screen for all the children in their class or group. This should be done in discussion with colleagues, in pairs or threes or at a staff meeting.

❖ Each screen is divided into three bands, and children are assessed band by band. This means that if children do not have all the skills in Band 1, they do not need to be assessed on Band 2, and if they do not have all the skills in Band 2, they do not need to be assessed on Band 3.

❖ A skill should be credited only if a child is using it *confidently*, *competently* and *consistently*. If there is any doubt or disagreement, or the child's use of the particular skill is irregular or infrequent, it should not be credited. At this stage it is better to underestimate children's abilities than overestimate them.

❖ Children who have all the skills in Bands 1 and 2 and at least one skill in Band 3 are identified as reasonably *Competent* in the relevant skills.

❖ Children who have all the skills in Band 1 and at least one skill in Band 2 are identified as *Developing* the relevant skills.

❖ All other children, that is, children who do not have all the skills in Band 1 and at least one skill in Band 2, are identified as *Delayed* in the relevant skills.

Note that children who do not have all the skills in Band 1 count as *Delayed* even if they have more than one skill in Band 2; and children who do not have all the skills in Band 2 still count as *Developing* even if they have more than one skill in Band 3.

At the *Conversation skills* and *Listening skills* steps in the programme, children identified as *Delayed* on the initial screen should be given intensive small-group work several times a week. Children identified as *Developing* or *Competent* in the relevant skills should also receive some small-group work if possible. (The preliminary step, *Getting started*, includes individual interaction with an adult for all children, and *Narrative skills* and *Discussion skills* provide partner or group work for all children in the class.)

The *Delayed* group may include some children with special educational needs but it should not be thought of as a special needs group. Children can be delayed for all sorts of reasons, including lack of confidence, lack of experience or lack of familiarity with the English language. Moreover, children identified as having special educational needs may be reasonably competent in some spoken language skills. They may, for example, be good at conversation but poor at listening. In any case, children whose spoken language is seriously affected by a special educational need will probably need additional support from a more detailed language programme such as *Teaching Talking* (Locke and Beech, 2005). See the section in Chapter 8 on children with special educational needs.

Using the skills checklists

At each main step of the programme there are three checklists for teaching to all children in the class. Each checklist includes a range of skills that it is reasonable to expect children to acquire over the course of a term, but this should be interpreted flexibly and adapted to the needs of the particular class or group. In particular, it is important not to rush through the first checklist in order to complete it by the end of the first term. If children are having difficulty with these basic skills they need to become competent and confident in them or they will have even more difficulty with later skills. It does not matter if some children do not complete the third checklist by the end of the year, but it is important that they all complete the second checklist.

The aim of the checklists is to guide and focus intervention by listing behaviours that can be taught one at a time, step by step. Each checklist is divided into groups of related sub-skills, in roughly developmental order, but children will typically develop these skills in parallel, and the rate and order of learning will differ from child to child. The content of the checklists sometimes overlaps too, because the skills themselves overlap and merge. This overlap and repetition provides useful reinforcement for previous learning.

Most children will show a pattern of skills from different parts of a checklist, and even from different checklists. That does not matter. Children's use of any of the skills should always be encouraged and reinforced whether or not it is the focus of current teaching, for example if some children are producing past tense narrative when the class is supposed to be concentrating on accounts in the present tense. But intervention should always concentrate on a specific skill from the checklist, to keep teaching focused and manageable and to ensure that all children in the class do learn it.

Procedure

❖ Staff should work through each checklist in turn, focusing on just a few items at a time. Each skill should be made an explicit teaching objective for one or more weeks, to ensure that all staff focus on that skill with all children and in all relevant activities, across the day and through the week.

❖ This can be a rolling programme of three or four skills at a time. That is, the class starts with one or two skills in the first week, adds another one or two in the second week, then replaces one or two with new skills in the third week, and so on.

❖ The sequence of skills in the checklist is meant only as a guide. Intervention should also be guided by the skills that children are developing spontaneously. In teaching one skill staff will often have been introducing another, and this can provide an easy transition from one skill to the next.

❖ Staff may find it helpful to identify in advance the skills they are going to teach and the order in which they are going to teach them, and build them into their advance planning so lessons can be prepared, resources gathered and support staff guided in their work with small groups or individual children. But planning needs to be flexible because some skills may take longer to learn than expected, and some weeks should be left free so that staff can go back and repeat or reinforce any skills that children have been finding difficult.

Procedure

❖ A list of the skills selected for current teaching should be displayed prominently in the classroom so all staff can refer to them and encourage and reinforce them at all times during the day.

Classroom intervention

One Step at a Time is implemented primarily through small-group work, supported by whole-class teaching and informal interaction during free activity sessions and daily classroom routines.

Small-group work

Children at the *Getting started* stage need individual attention to develop their confidence and basic communication skills but at later stages group work is the most efficient way of teaching and monitoring individual children (the *Narrative skills* programme uses partner work instead of small groups). It is however important that these be *small* groups. 'Group work' can sometimes mean as many as 10–12 children. For work on spoken language there should be no more than four to six children in the group. Many children find it difficult to understand or concentrate in large groups. In a smaller group they can follow and join in, the teacher can relate to each child in turn, and other children in the group will learn from the exchange. Groups also need to be small to ensure that all children participate, and to monitor individual learning. In a larger group it is easy for some children to escape notice. Video evidence shows that while staff may feel that the children have never stopped talking, some have actually said nothing and show very little awareness of what is going on.

Ideally, intensive small-group work should be provided for all children, but when resources are limited – as they usually are – priority must be given first to children identified as *Delayed* and then to children identified as *Developing*. Children identified as *Competent* should also be given small-group work if at all possible. Small-group activities prove surprisingly popular and these children may feel disappointed or left out if they are not given their own 'special time' with a member of staff. The programmes in Years 1 and 2 do provide partner or small-group work for all children in the class, but staff will still need to work more closely with those children identified as *Delayed* or *Developing*.

Whole-class teaching

Whole-class lessons are used to support this small-group work. They are needed to introduce, demonstrate and explain new skills, activities and vocabulary; to practise, reinforce and generalize children's learning; and to ensure that all children in the class, not just those identified as *Delayed* or *Developing*, get experience and practice in the relevant skills.

New items for teaching should first be introduced in a separate whole-class lesson, but subsequent whole-class work does not need to be in separate or special language lessons. Instead, the skills and vocabulary that children are currently learning can be, and should be, featured in any lesson, at any time, several times a day. This gives children valuable experience of the relevant skills and vocabulary being used in different situations and contexts, and by other children as well as adults. Circle-time, talk-time and story-time are the most obvious opportunities for working on language skills but curriculum lessons and physical activities such as playground games, art and design, PE and music also provide suitable occasions.

Classroom activities and daily routines

The everyday activities of coming into or leaving the classroom, lining up, putting on outdoor clothes or taking them off, preparing for lessons and clearing away afterwards, all provide good opportunities for informal conversation where staff can reinforce and monitor the learning of individual children. All staff should be made aware of the skills or words of the week, and introduce, encourage and reward them with individual children, pairs and groups whenever they can.

Procedure

❖ Each skill should be introduced, explained and/or demonstrated to the class or group as a whole before being made the focus of small-group or partner work. When introducing any new skill or activity it is always good practice to explain what it is that children need to learn and why they need to learn it. If children know what is expected of them they are much more likely to exhibit the behaviour in question.

❖ There should then be at least one whole-class activity every day focusing on the skills currently being learned. These need not take place in separate or special lessons – they can be used in curriculum lessons, circle-time or story-time; in activities such as playground games, art and design, PE or music – but the class teacher should identify at least one specific occasion each day when staff will model, encourage and reinforce the relevant skills for all children, not just for those receiving small-group work.

❖ All staff should be encouraged to use every other opportunity through the day, including playtime and dinnertime, to model, encourage and reinforce these skills with individual children.

Small-group work

❖ Each group should be of four to six children. As far as possible, the same member of staff should always lead each group.

❖ Children identified as *Delayed* should be given 10–15 minutes small-group work every day if possible, certainly two or three times a week. Children identified as *Developing* should be given 10–15 minutes small-group work at least once a week. Children identified as *Competent* should also be given small-group work wherever possible.

❖ It is usually convenient to group the children identified as *Delayed*, and the children identified as *Developing*, because that is easier to schedule and makes it easier to support and monitor the children most in need of it. But children will also benefit from mixed-ability groupings. Absences can give opportunities to include *Competent* or *Developing* children in the *Developing* or *Delayed* groups.

Procedure

❖ The same groupings can be used as for other purposes but language teaching should be additional to other small-group work. Groups can be reorganized if children progress at different rates through the year.

❖ Small-group teaching should proceed at a pace that includes every child. It is better to consolidate a skill for all children than to push ahead too quickly. It does not matter if children are learning at different rates; all children will benefit from the extra practice. However if some children are still learning a skill after three or more weeks, it may be sensible to leave it for a while and come back to it again later.

❖ Teaching a particular skill should normally continue until all the children in that group have learned it, but if one or two children are having particular difficulty they should not delay the rest. They will need whatever additional support the school can provide. If several children in the class are having difficulty it may be necessary to continue teaching that skill to these children, and possibly to the whole class, for longer than originally planned.

Lesson planning

Lesson planning includes setting objectives, selecting activities and preparing materials. In *One Step at a Time* teaching and learning objectives are provided by the skill checklists and vocabulary word lists but, because spoken language teaching needs to be integrated with the rest of the curriculum, it should not usually be necessary to plan new activities or prepare different materials. Staff should instead look to the activities and materials that they are already using and consider how they can be used to develop the skills and vocabulary that they have set as their teaching objectives. Some suggestions for appropriate activities are given in Chapters 9–13, including the detailed notes on each checklist. Some examples of planning sheets, based on the actual planning of schools that have been piloting the programme, are given in Appendix 3.

Teaching method

As described in Chapter 3, there is more to learning spoken language than merely being exposed to adult models. We actually teach children how to talk, and how to listen, without quite realizing we are doing it. We do this by:

◆ providing a model, at the right level, for the child to copy. The language we use is based on the language the child is using himself or seems to understand. Often we simply take what the child has just said and repeat it back to him, adding more words or extra complexity: 'That's right. It's a boat. It's a big boat.';

◆ emphasizing or highlighting the particular words or expressions we want the child to learn. With babies in particular we seem to say almost everything twice;

- encouraging the child to respond, prompting him with nods, smiles or questions;
- rewarding any response with smiles, praise and further encouragement. A positive response from the adult seems to be a reward in itself.

These are also the techniques we need to use, explicitly and systematically, for teaching spoken language in schools.

- *Modelling*: the adult demonstrates the skill she wants children to learn, for example she claps in time to the music or shows how to tell a story 'in your own words', and encourages them to copy her example. Imitation is a powerful means of teaching and learning.

- *Highlighting*: the adult draws attention to the relevant skill by discussing it, emphasizing its importance, or explaining how, when or why we use it, for example why we should look at someone when they are speaking to us, why it is difficult to follow a complex instruction, or how we can reach agreement in a discussion. She can do this by asking questions like 'What do we say when someone comes to visit us?' and 'What can you do if you don't understand?' Then she discusses the children's responses, summarizing and highlighting the key points: 'So what do we do when someone comes into our classroom? We look at them, we smile and we say "Hello".'

- *Prompting*: the adult encourages the child to respond, directing him towards the appropriate behaviour: 'What is this called?' … 'Can you tell me some more about that?' … 'What happened then?' … 'Show me how can you can march in time to this music.' … 'What do you think the boy is going to do now?' … 'Does that seem a good idea?'

- *Rewarding*: the adult rewards appropriate responses with praise and further encouragement. Children should always be encouraged to respond, but indiscriminate praise – praising anything and everything they say or do – will not help them to learn. If the praise can emphasize what was good about the response – 'What a good question!' … 'You *were* listening well.' … 'That was a good idea you and Steve worked out together.' – it will help children recognize what it is you want them to learn. If a response is not quite what the adult is looking for, she can encourage a more appropriate one by asking questions, prompting or modelling the skill again. This should be supportive and non-judgemental, encouraging a better, more confident or more mature response. It should not be negative or dismissive.

These techniques are the basis of all language teaching. They can be used for teaching vocabulary and grammar, and for teaching skills and uses. They can be used in one-to-one intervention, in small-group work and in whole-class lessons. Parents use them naturally, without noticing what they are doing, but teachers need to be explicitly aware of them. Before starting a checklist, staff will find it useful to go over the various behaviours together and discuss how they can model, highlight, prompt and reward them.

Reviewing progress and moving on

Ideally all children should be monitored as they acquire each skill, but in practice staff will probably have to concentrate on the children classified as *Delayed*, with some additional support for those identified as *Developing*. It should not usually be necessary to monitor children who have been identified as *Competent*. Individual monitoring is particularly important in nursery and Reception (children aged 3 to 5) because this is the time when children are establishing basic competences and those who fall behind at this stage may never catch up.

It is, however, important that staff also make time to observe all the children in their class or group, not just those identified as *Delayed*, to see what skills they are using spontaneously. The pressure to keep moving through the curriculum is so great that staff may find this difficult, but they can learn as much about children's spoken language from informal observation as from formal monitoring. This is also the best way of ensuring that children have been placed in the correct categories of *Competent*, *Developing* or *Delayed*.

Procedure

❖ Staff can keep a running record of individual progress by entering children's names on the checklist and ticking off each skill as each child acquires it. A skill should not be credited until the child is using it *confidently*, *competently* and *consistently*.

❖ Staff should also review all children at the end of the term or the beginning of the next term, to bring records up to date and possibly reorganize teaching groups or move some children from one category to another. Teaching groups can also be reconsidered when starting a new checklist.

❖ Ideally, teaching of each checklist should continue until every child in the group or class has acquired all the skills on that checklist. This may not be possible by the end of term, in which case teaching of that checklist can continue into the next term.

At the end of the year

❖ Ideally, all children will at least have completed the second checklist by the end of the year. Children who are still very delayed at the end of the year may need special provision, such as further small-group work in the relevant skills, either in their current class or by returning to the previous year's class for some lessons.

❖ If a significant number of children have not completed the second checklist, or have barely begun the third, it may be sensible to continue teaching the current programme into the first term of the following year, and not introduce the next step until the second term.

❖ Staff should in any case liaise with staff for the following year and pass on the details of children who have not completed checklists, their likely progress, and any further support they may need.

See also the section on children who do not complete a step by the end of the year in Chapter 8.

7

Teaching vocabulary

Vocabulary is clearly essential for language. Without vocabulary we would have no language at all. Vocabulary also seems to be the motor of grammatical development. The more words that children know, and the more different types of word they know, the sooner they develop grammatical forms. It is easy to think that 'vocabulary' means nouns, verbs and adjectives, but children also need to learn adverbs, prepositions and connectives like *if*, *because* and *although*, both to understand the sentences they hear and read, and to add variety and structure to their own sentences. Children with a limited vocabulary will have a limited sentence structure as well.

Vocabulary is equally crucial for learning. The more words that children understand, the more they will learn from others and from what they read. The more words they can use for themselves, the more they can establish and extend their learning, for example by answering questions and by asking them. If they don't have the vocabulary they won't know how to answer or what to ask. The words that we know also affect what we can think, and even what we observe in the world around us. The Inuit who learn several different words for different kinds of snow are, at the same time, learning to notice the different kinds of snow that those words name. The more words we know, and the more precise and detailed those words are, the more information we can convey and the more precise and detailed that information will be.

Vocabulary is also crucial for teaching. It's not just that we use words to teach with. We use them to bring the outside world into the classroom. Early learning is based on physical activity with physical objects – touching things, playing with them, exploring them – and even when children enter school or nursery, handling things is still the best way of learning. But at school children also have to be able to learn without having the thing in front of them, without being able to manipulate it for themselves. We cannot bring everything into the classroom, so we teach children about the world by using words that stand for the things outside. Even if we use pictures, photographs or drawings, we teach by talking about them. The more words that children know, the more we can teach them, and the more we can teach them about.

Spoken vocabulary also contributes to literacy by enabling children to understand what they read, both directly because they know what the words mean, and indirectly in that the bigger their vocabulary, the better they will be at grasping the meaning of a passage as a whole and therefore at guessing the meaning of the words they do not know. These words can then be added to their vocabulary. Vocabulary also gives them the resources for independent writing. The wider children's vocabulary, the more accurate, detailed and complex their writing can be.

The link between vocabulary and literacy should be obvious. The link between vocabulary and other curriculum subjects may be less so. Children need the relevant vocabulary to understand new subjects and topics, and the wider their vocabulary, the deeper their understanding will be. Here, too, they need to know not just the crucial nouns, verbs and adjectives, but also the adverbs, prepositions and connectives that provide detail, structure and insight. 'Articulate vocabulary is not simply a gloss to improve the appearance of students' work,' writes a secondary history teacher (Woodcock, 2005), 'but a fundamental tool with which to develop conceptual understanding.'

> *Words are tools, not just for speaking and writing but also for thought and developing new ideas ... In order to develop students' understanding of the Second World War, I experimented with providing them with new vocabulary, which they would not otherwise have known or chosen to use ... By encouraging them to consider the deep, varied meanings and implications of words, I hoped to introduce new ideas, new ways of thinking about events, and new means of expressing subtle, precise ideas.*
>
> J. Woodcock (2005), 'Latent meaning', *Times Educational Supplement*, 18 November 2005, reprinted by kind permission of the author

Vocabulary is also an important element in what is sometimes called emotional literacy or emotional intelligence. This involves a number of things, including the ability to understand your own feelings and communicate them appropriately, and the ability to recognize and respond to the feelings of others and interpret their behaviour. To achieve this, and to use this understanding to manage their feelings and control their behaviour, children need to have the vocabulary to identify and discuss a variety of different feelings and emotions, both positive and negative.

Finally, the more teachers highlight vocabulary and teach it explicitly, the more children will become aware of words and the role that they play in their learning, and of their own vocabulary knowledge. This helps children to appreciate the importance of finding out the meanings of any words or expressions they don't understand, not only in their reading, but also in other subjects too.

Vocabulary is, however, easy to take for granted. It is easy to assume that children already know the words used to introduce a new topic or subject or the simple, basic words like *in* or *on* that classroom teaching depends on. But vocabulary that seems obvious to adults may not always be familiar to children. A child who ignores an instruction to put something away may not be being stubborn or naughty; he simply may not understand the expression *put it away*.

There are, moreover, two aspects to 'knowing' a word or phrase: understanding it when it is used by others (comprehension) and being able to use it correctly yourself (expression). Children need to be able to do both: they need to understand words and sentences, and they need to be able to produce them for themselves. Understanding usually comes before use. Parents are sometimes astonished at how much their toddlers understand, long before they start speaking. It's the same when adults are learning another language: they can understand what other people are saying to them even if they can't or don't remember how to say it themselves.

Understanding is particularly easy to take for granted. It is all too easy for teachers to use language that is too complex or too sophisticated for the children they are talking to. It is also difficult to assess because children who seem to understand may simply be copying other children. The simplest guide to understanding is if children can use the words appropriately for themselves, but even here they may be copying other people. Some children say a lot without really understanding what they are saying.

It is, however, unrealistic to expect staff to assess children's vocabulary once they have got beyond a few basic words. Instead they need to decide what words they think the children in their class need to know, and use them as the basis of intervention and monitoring. *One Step at a Time* concentrates on four key types of vocabulary (see Chapter 2):

- ◆ basic vocabulary
- ◆ early cross-curricular vocabulary
- ◆ the vocabulary of feelings and emotion
- ◆ essential curriculum vocabulary.

Vocabulary wordlists

One Step at a Time provides at each step of the programme a list of 100 key words for explicit teaching and monitoring. For *Getting started* it is a 'starter' vocabulary of the 100 words that children are most likely to learn first. For *Conversation skills*, *Listening skills* and *Narrative skills* it is a combination of early cross-curricular vocabulary and the vocabulary of feelings and emotion. For *Discussion skills* it is the vocabulary of discussion, agreement and negotiation, including words for feelings and emotion.

As well as these 100 specified words, staff should also include any essential curriculum vocabulary from the subjects and topics they are currently teaching. Before introducing a new topic they should first identify the key words that children in their class will need to know, that is, the words that name or describe the things they will be learning about. The children themselves can be included in this process, to see which items of key vocabulary are already familiar and which need to be explained or taught to them. Talking about the words will be talking about the topic, and vice versa, and as well as identifying any words that need to be taught, the discussion will help children to reflect on their own vocabulary and understand why it matters, how words are important and why they need to know them.

Classroom intervention

All vocabulary items chosen for teaching need to be introduced and explained to all children in the class, especially the prepositions and other words that are common to many subjects and activities and can easily be forgotten or taken for granted. After that, curriculum vocabulary can be taught as part of normal curriculum teaching; adjectives, prepositions and adverbs can be taught in curriculum lessons or during activities of various sorts; and the vocabulary of feelings and emotion can often be taught in the context of stories or when discussing classroom or playground incidents.

Procedure

❖ Staff should identify 6–10 words for teaching each week as 'this week's special words'. As well as words chosen from current curriculum topics, they should include between two and four words from the *One Step at a Time* vocabulary lists. If children are finding some words difficult they can be featured over several weeks, or repeated at different times during the year.

❖ It will usually be convenient to teach a selection of words from the same category (quality, colour, etc.) at the same time, but staff should avoid words that are similar in sound or meaning (for example *big* and *biggest*, *loud* and *noisy*) and contrasting pairs (for example *black* and *white*, *quick* and *slow*), which some children will find confusing.

❖ The words for the week should be introduced and explained to the whole class at the beginning of the week, and displayed prominently in the classroom for reference by children as well as staff.

❖ These words should then be included and featured by all staff on every possible occasion over the rest of the week, in whole-class lessons, group work, one-to-one interaction and classroom routines. Children who have begun to read can support their own learning by being encouraged to consult the list of this week's words, look out for them in their lessons and reading, and use them in their own talk and writing.

Teaching method

The basic techniques for teaching vocabulary are the same as for other language skills (see Chapter 6):

◆ modelling

◆ highlighting

◆ prompting

◆ rewarding.

However, the key to vocabulary learning is having frequent opportunities to hear the word used in context and then to use it for yourself. This involves four steps:

◆ experience of the object, activity or characteristic that is being named or described. If these are unfamiliar, children will have to get used to and understand them before they can grasp the meanings of the words;

◆ understanding the word as used by others;

◆ being able to use the word when prompted or encouraged, for example by being asked to name something or being given a sentence to complete: 'That is your … (sock)';

◆ using the word spontaneously.

Older or more able children may do this very quickly, almost simultaneously. Other children may learn much more slowly. Especially with more abstract terms there can be quite a long time between children understanding the words and starting to use them for themselves.

Young children will find it easier to learn vocabulary by being actively involved with familiar real objects including toys rather than looking at books or pictures. So when the teacher introduces 'this week's special words' at the start of the week she should demonstrate their meaning using familiar activities and objects that the children can handle. Then there should be opportunities every day for the children to repeat these activities for themselves. Physical activity seems particularly important in grasping prepositions, spatial concepts and other words needed for the early years curriculum, including terms of position (*in, off, under*), movement (*through, backwards, away*) and quantity and quality (*some, again, small, heavy*). When children are beginning to use the word staff can introduce less familiar contexts, and pictures as well as real objects, to extend and consolidate their learning.

Older children can be taught vocabulary in groups or whole-class lessons. Staff should then find or create opportunities to highlight these words in other activities, for example story-time, talk-time or circle-time. They will also find it useful to build up a stock of material to illustrate relevant vocabulary, such as pictures from shopping catalogues (especially children's catalogues), computer Clip Art and photographs, especially photos of the children themselves. It will also be useful to identify a set of stories to illustrate various feeling and emotion words and other words like *night-time* or *birthday*.

Concrete nouns and verbs

New words should be taught using a few familiar objects and situations at first. Other situations and objects can be introduced when children show that they understand the word by responding appropriately to questions and instructions. Children who are talking confidently and frequently can be encouraged to use the word for themselves by prompting them with questions or open-ended comments, but young children should not be pressured into actually using the words.

Adjectives, prepositions and adverbs

The simplest and most obvious way to teach an adjective is by comparing and contrasting an object or activity that illustrates the property with something that doesn't, for example contrasting something that is *noisy* with something that is *not noisy*. But with young children it is important not to introduce the opposite term at the same time, that is not to contrast *noisy* with *quiet*, because they will find it confusing having to learn both words at once. The opposite term, in this case *quiet*, should not be introduced until some weeks or months later, and it too should be taught by contrasting it with *not quiet*, not with *noisy*. Opposites should only be introduced together when both words have been established separately.

Older children should be better able to grasp contrasting pairs like *solid* and *hollow* or *equal* and *unequal*, but it is still best not to introduce both words at the same time. Instead, the teacher should teach *equal* first, without using *unequal* (she can use *not equal* instead), and then use *equal* later when she is teaching *unequal*. Older children should also be able to understand comparatives (*rougher, smaller*) and superlatives (*longest, heaviest*), though the teacher should take time to discuss and explain these ideas.

Prepositions and adverbs are best taught through movement and activity, by climbing *under* something, putting one thing *inside* another, or moving something *slowly* or *backwards*. PE and games, or circle-time, provide good opportunities for teaching these words.

More abstract words, and the vocabulary of feelings and emotion

More abstract words like *number*, *soon* or *today* and the vocabulary of feelings and emotion need a slightly different approach. The teacher should begin by asking questions like 'Who knows what a *number* is?' … 'Who knows what *thirsty* means?' … 'When do people get *frightened*?' or 'What does it mean if we are going to do something *soon*?' She can then build on the answers to explain and develop the concept at a level the children will understand. If there are no appropriate responses the teacher will have to explain the term herself using familiar activities or situations, and then help the children to produce their own examples as a basis for further discussion.

With the vocabulary of feelings and emotion it is also important to highlight the types of context in which the feeling occurs ('Would you be afraid of a tiger?') and the physical response, both the internal feeling ('You go all tight in your tummy.') and any overt behaviour ('Do you want to hide?'), to help children identify and understand what they are feeling. With these words in particular, teachers should take a few minutes every day to go over again with the class what they mean, what they involve, and any new instances that may have occurred. She should also look for or create opportunities to highlight the word in other activities every day, for example by selecting an appropriate story for the week, to illustrate that emotion.

As these words are likely to be particularly difficult, staff should look for understanding but not insist that children use them for themselves. It is also sensible to put aside a week or two at the end of the term or half-term to go back over the words that have been taught so far, as well as any other words that children have been slow to learn.

Reviewing progress and moving on

Ideally, all vocabulary learning will be monitored individually but in practice staff will probably have to concentrate on those children who seem to be slow in acquiring new vocabulary. This will probably include the children whose language skills have been identified as *Delayed*, but there may be other children whose vocabulary or grammar are inadequate for their age or who seem to be having difficulty for other reasons. These children should, if possible, be assessed or monitored on their own because, when working in groups, it is easy to miss some children, especially those who are quiet, though talkative children may also know less than they seem to.

The best way to assess and monitor vocabulary is through one-to-one conversation. In conversation, staff can introduce the word, observe the child's responses, encourage him to use it for himself and check that he is using it appropriately. But although this detailed monitoring may be possible in nurseries with a good adult–child ratio, it becomes increasingly difficult as children move into larger classes. So (except for *Getting started*) it is suggested that staff concentrate on understanding. The crucial thing is that children understand the language that staff are using, and when they understand a word they will normally start using it themselves.

Understanding can be checked by asking questions, giving instructions and seeing if children respond appropriately, or by using objects or pictures and getting children to point to or select the *red* flower, the *little* bear, the *square* shape, the *flat* stone, the *biggest* box, something *shiny*, etc. Pictures are not recommended for teaching early vocabulary, but they are useful for checking understanding, precisely because children find them more difficult. If pictures are used for consolidating and generalizing learning as described above, a different set of pictures should be used for checking understanding.

Procedure

❖ Towards the end of the week staff should monitor the learning of all children and identify any words that seem to be proving particularly difficult. Children who are slow in acquiring new vocabulary should be checked individually.

❖ The crucial test is that these children understand the word in question, whether or not they are using it (they may be copying other children). Understanding can be checked by asking questions, or by giving instructions and seeing if children respond appropriately, while making sure that they are not following other children.

❖ Children who have difficulty learning new vocabulary can be put in groups of four to six children for additional small-group vocabulary lessons. The words they need to learn can be entered on a *Vocabulary checklist* (Appendix 2) and ticked off as each child learns them.

❖ Teaching each word should normally continue until all children in the group have learned it (in the early years this may take several weeks). It does not matter if children are learning at different rates; these children will benefit from the extra practice. But if one or two children are having particular difficulty they should not delay the rest. They will need to be given whatever additional support the school or nursery can provide.

8

Managing the programme

This chapter discusses a number of detailed issues that may arise in using *One Step at a Time*, including introducing the programme into a school or nursery, training and inducting staff, involving parents, or working with children who develop more slowly than other children in the class and do not complete checklists by the end of the year.

Introducing *One Step at a Time* into a school or nursery

One Step at a Time is designed as a cumulative programme in which each year builds on skills acquired in the previous year. So it, too, is best introduced one step at a time; it is not meant to be introduced in all four years at once. This is partly because children in later years will not have been through the earlier steps in the programme, but also to allow schools to work themselves into the programme gradually without overstretching staff or other resources.

Similarly, where staff are teaching a mixture of age groups in the same class, for example both nursery and Reception children, or a combination of Years 1 and 2, it will be sensible to introduce the same step for all children in the first year and not try to introduce differentiated teaching (for example *Conversation skills* with the nursery children and *Listening skills* with the Reception children) until the second year.

Nevertheless, some schools will be eager to get started! Schools with a nursery may want to introduce *Listening skills* into Reception at the same time as they introduce *Conversation skills* (with or without *Getting started*) into the nursery year. Some schools without a nursery may want to introduce *Narrative skills* into Year 1 at the same time as they introduce *Listening skills* into Reception. In that case the advice below to treat the first year as a learning period and not to feel under pressure to implement everything at once is particularly relevant. In particular, staff may have to proceed more slowly with the classes that have not done previous steps in the programme.

It is, however, not advisable to introduce *Conversation skills*, *Listening skills* and *Narrative skills* into all three years at once, or for Year 2 children to do *Discussion skills* without having done *Narrative skills*. Children in subsequent years will benefit from discussion work and may be able to handle this step in the programme without having done the other steps. But group discussion without adult support puts considerable demands on children's social and linguistic skills, and if there is any doubt about their ability to work constructively in small discussion groups it is better to begin with paired or partner work on narrative skills as described in Chapter 12. Schools can either omit *Discussion skills* in the first year they use the programme and not introduce them until the following year, when the Year 2 children will have done *Narrative skills*; or they can use *Narrative skills* in both Year 1 and Year 2 for that first year and not introduce *Discussion skills* into Year 2 until the following year.

The first year

The first year of using *One Step at a Time* should be seen as a learning period for staff as well as – or even more than – the children. In recent years schools and nurseries have been overwhelmed by a large number of new initiatives – more than 160 at the latest count. These have usually been accompanied by a great deal of advice and information on how to implement the new programme or strategy, that is, on what staff are expected to do and what children are expected to achieve. Less attention is given to whether staff have the necessary expertise or training to implement the new programme successfully. But if initial training is inadequate or non-existent – as is often the case with spoken language – staff will need time to learn new techniques and familiarize themselves with new procedures. The pressure is always on producing results as quickly as possible, but concentrating on children's progress and achievement is starting in the wrong place. Children are unlikely to benefit until staff have become skilled and confident in what they have to do. And, as any experienced member of staff will tell you, that takes time.

This applies equally when schools or nurseries are introducing the programme for the first time; when staff are new to a school or class in which the programme is already running; or when an existing member of staff moves to a class at a stage of the programme that is new to her. The first year should be a time for staff to familiarize themselves with the programme and its procedures, adapt it to their needs and purposes, and build up suitable teaching activities and resources. Experience shows that all staff learn a great deal about children's spoken language in the first year of using the programme, and if they are learning, the children will be learning too.

In particular, staff should not be concerned if they do not manage to implement a whole step of the programme in the first year. For example, they might want to concentrate on skills teaching, and not introduce vocabulary teaching until the second year. They should also not feel the need to go any faster than is comfortable for themselves as well as the children in their class or group.

The staff co-ordinator

All schools and nurseries using the programme should appoint an existing member of staff to co-ordinate its implementation in the nursery or across the school. If the programme has been running for a while, this should be someone with personal experience of using it, preferably at more than one level. Where a number of nurseries feed into a primary school without a nursery year, a member of staff from the primary school can be appointed as co-ordinator to work with all the nurseries involved.

The staff co-ordinator should be responsible for training existing staff, inducting new staff, advising on teaching methods and materials, involving parents, answering queries and dealing with problems, and networking with other schools or nurseries using the programme. She should start by making herself thoroughly familiar with *One Step at a Time*, including the background chapters.

Schools and nurseries have benefited enormously from working closely with other schools or nurseries that are introducing the same steps in the programme or, even better, are already experienced in using them. Where a group of schools and/or nurseries are working particularly closely together it may be desirable to appoint a co-ordinator responsible for training, networking, etc., across the whole cluster, or perhaps a separate co-ordinator for each year of the programme.

Training and induction

All staff using *One Step at a Time*, including support staff, have some in-service training. It can be delivered by the staff co-ordinator or, in later years, by staff experienced in using the various steps of the programme, and should include:

- the methodology and structure of *One Step at a Time* (Chapters 2 to 7);
- the procedures and teaching method for each step in the programme (Chapters 9 to 13).

This last will be different for staff working at different steps of the programme, but it is important for everyone to know how the step they are teaching fits into the wider programme and which skills or vocabulary children will have covered already or will learn in later years.

Training can also usefully include:

- the importance of spoken language and its role in learning, literacy and social and emotional development (Chapter 1);

- the development of spoken language from birth through childhood to 9 years (Appendix 1).

It is important not to take training for granted, even in nurseries or schools where the programme is well established. Obviously, all staff will need some training in the first year of using the programme, but training also needs to be repeated in later years for staff who are new to the school, new to the programme or moving from one year to another. Given the amount of staff movement in the typical primary school, some of it at the last moment, training will normally have to be repeated every year. Because the start of the school year is always a busy time, as much training as possible should be given at the end of the previous year. Wherever possible, training can be shared with other schools or nurseries using the programme.

Networking

In an area where several schools or nurseries are using the programme, staff will find it very helpful to share their experiences and expertise with colleagues from other schools. Experienced staff always have a great deal to teach their less experienced colleagues! Each step of the programme should have its own networking group, with:

◆ opportunities for staff to visit other schools or nurseries where their step of the programme is operating, not just in initial training but also in the first year or two that they are using that step themselves;

◆ regular meetings for all staff working at the same level of the programme, for mutual advice and support, and to share ideas about planning and teaching methods, materials and activities.

Networking groups should meet once a term in the first year of using the programme, and at least once a year thereafter.

Children who have not done previous steps of the programme

There will always be some children who have not done the previous steps in the programme, for example because they have come from another school. They will have to be fitted in with the rest of the class and given whatever additional support they need and the school can provide. They may also need to be assessed using screens from the previous years.

Schools without a nursery

In schools without a nursery it is likely that many or all children entering Reception will not have done *Conversation skills*. In that case Reception staff should first complete the *Conversation skills* screen with all children. Children identified as *Competent* in *Conversation skills* can be regarded as ready for *Listening skills* and can go on to the *Listening skills* initial screen. But children identified as *Developing* in *Conversation skills* are going to need more work on their conversation, and children identified as *Delayed* in *Conversation skills* will have to be regarded as being back at the *Getting started* stage. What happens next depends on the numbers involved.

Hopefully, most children in the class will be ready for *Listening skills*. In that case whole-class work can focus on listening skills, supported by small-group work for children identified as *Developing* or *Delayed* in those skills. However, children identified as *Developing* or *Delayed* in *Conversation skills* will need small-group work from the *Conversation skills* or *Getting started* programmes, supported, wherever possible, by whole-class and other activities. These children will benefit from whole-class listening work, but their intensive small-group work should be focused on the earlier programmes. In other words, staff will need to run these programmes in parallel.

At the end of the first term or the following half-term these children can be reassessed on the *Conversation skills* initial screen in the hope that they will now be ready to move on to the *Listening skills* programme. But they will still be behind other children in their class, and any children who are not ready to move up by the middle of the second term will be even further behind. This is discussed further below.

However if a large number of Reception children are identified as *Developing* or *Delayed* in *Conversation skills* it may be more sensible to do that in Reception, *Listening skills* in Year 1, and so on, through to *Discussion skills* in Year 3. Schools in disadvantaged areas may feel that this is more realistic in any case, without needing to screen individual children. But they need to recognize that *One Step at a Time* puts *Listening skills* in the Reception year because they are crucial for the development of reading, so schools that delay *Listening skills* until Year 1 will need to think about delaying their reading programmes. And it is similar with *Narrative skills* and writing. The fact is that some children need this extra experience before they will be ready for literacy, but schools may have to explain and justify this decision to parents and others.

Children from *Getting started* who do not complete *Conversation skills* by the end of the year

Some children on the *Getting started* programme will move up to *Conversation skills* during the nursery year, and be ready to begin *Listening skills* in Reception. Others will not. Some may not complete *Conversation skills* during the nursery year (that is, not complete the second checklist by the end of the year); some may not even complete *Getting started*; and some schools may have large numbers of these children. Again the alternatives are to run *Conversation* and *Listening skills* in tandem, or to delay *Conversation skills* until the Reception year, as described above.

Other children who do not complete a step by the end of the year

The skills featured in *One Step at a Time* continue to develop throughout childhood, through primary and secondary school and beyond. The aim of the programme is to provide sufficient initial practice that children can continue to learn and develop these skills from what goes on in school and their interaction with other children. Without this initial experience and practice, children who are behind to start with will fall even further behind.

However, some children may not reach the point where they are self-sufficient in acquiring these skills, even with the benefit of the programme. In terms of the programme, these will be children who do not complete the relevant step (that is, do not complete the second checklist) by the end of the appropriate year. The school will have to give these children whatever additional support it can provide. Many of them are likely to need this support in the long term; some will have been identified as having special educational needs. In terms of the programme this further support should include continuing work on the previous steps. For example, children who do not complete *Listening skills* in Reception should be given further practice in *Listening skills* in Year 1, possibly involving staff from Reception, or taking these children out of Year 1 for small-group work in Reception. Alternatively, it might be a school decision for some children to repeat the Reception year.

If a significant number of children have not completed the second checklist, or have barely begun the third checklist, it may be sensible to continue teaching the current programme into the first term of the following year and not to introduce the next step until the second term.

Children for whom English is an additional language

Children may be classified as *Delayed* on the initial screens for all sorts of reasons. For some it will be because English is not their home language. *One Step at a Time* will be equally effective with these children. *Getting started*, in particular, can be very useful in developing both language and confidence in children whose knowledge of English is very limited or who find school a strange and frightening experience. Older children with very limited English will also benefit from working through the *Starter vocabulary*, which is part of the *Getting started* programme.

Most of these children will improve rapidly and, once started, should progress through the programme more quickly than *Delayed* English-speaking children. But some of them may also be *Delayed* in their home language. For this reason it will be very helpful if the programme can be operated in their home language as well as in English, either by using home-language speakers in the classroom or by involving their parents. This will indicate whether any apparent delay is just in English or in spoken language more generally. There may be concern that working in two languages at the same time will confuse these children, but the evidence is that while children learning more than one language may be slightly slower than other children in establishing either language, in the longer term their spoken language actually benefits from stimulation in separate languages.

Children with special educational needs

A special educational need can affect children's spoken language either directly, in that it is or includes a difficulty specifically with language or communication (for example specific language impairment or autistic spectrum difficulties), or indirectly, in that it affects the acquisition of spoken language (for example visual or auditory impairments). *One Step at a Time* should be very effective with the latter group, but children who have difficulties specifically with language or communication may have to proceed much more slowly than other children in the class. With these children it may be useful to indicate on the checklists not just when they are using a skill confidently, competently and consistently, but also when they are beginning to develop it. Staff can do this by, for example, putting a dot in the tick box when a skill is first noticed, or using one tick for a skill that is only emerging or inconsistent and two ticks for one that has been firmly established.

Children with significant difficulties will benefit from the *Getting started* level of the programme but may be slow to develop more advanced skills. Schools will have their own policies and procedures for supporting these children, tailored to the particular needs of the individual child. They should be included in whole-class and small-group spoken language work as far as is possible and practicable without putting them under unnecessary pressure or delaying other children in the class. They can also be given individual support by using a personalized spoken language programme like *Teaching Talking* (Locke and Beech, 2005).

Teaching Talking operates at three levels: identification and initial support, using initial screens and classroom strategies; small-group intervention, using language records and small-group language work; and detailed profiling, using detailed profiles and individual intervention. These correspond to the pre-SEN level and the 'Action' and 'Action Plus' levels in the revised *Special Educational Needs Code of Practice* for England and Wales (DfES, 2001) and can be used to plan intervention in accordance with the code of practice.

Children who are doing *One Step at a Time* will already be doing small-group language work but the *Teaching Talking* language records will help to provide an individual education plan. The detailed profiles will be particularly useful for children needing individual intervention because they assess several areas of development, not just spoken language. The Procedures Handbook, the Activities Handbook and the Detailed Profiles from *Teaching Talking* can all be purchased separately.

Children with unclear speech

A particular problem in the early years may be children whose speech is difficult or even impossible to understand. This is a common problem because at the age of three, when most children now enter school or nursery, they are still establishing the full range of speech sounds. Delay in establishing a few sounds and some other difficulties like a tendency to stammer, hesitate or repeat when excited, should not be regarded as a cause for concern. Older children with unclear speech should be referred to a speech and language therapist if possible.

The important thing with these children is not to make an issue of their speech. Staff should not correct them, make them repeat themselves or otherwise embarrass them, but should speak slowly and carefully, providing good, clear models of correct speech, and generally support and encourage them, and build their self-esteem if they seem shy or nervous. It may also be sensible to check their hearing, because poor speech may be the result of undiagnosed poor hearing. This can be done through informal observation, by noticing how they respond in noisy surroundings or speaking in a soft voice and noting their reaction.

Children whose speech is almost incomprehensible should also be referred to a speech and language therapist as soon as possible. School staff should not try to work directly on these children's speech without expert advice or guidance but it is important to establish some means of communication. Nothing is more stressful for teacher and child than not being able to understand each other. The most useful thing is to listen to these children as much as possible, remembering the importance of context and activity as a way of both encouraging them to talk and interpreting what they say. Their speech usually becomes more comprehensible with familiarity. Other children may be better at understanding them and able to interpret for them.

All these children will be helped by the listening activities described in Chapter 11. For further information and advice on children with unclear speech see the Procedures Handbook in *Teaching Talking* (Locke and Beech, 2005), Chapters 2 and 6.

Involving parents

Parents can be involved and included in *One Step at a Time* in two ways: by supporting their child's learning at home and/or by helping out in the school or nursery itself. Although the two are separate, parents who help out in the school or nursery will become more aware of what they can do to help their own children at home.

Chapter 3 outlined a number of elements in natural language learning that are difficult to reproduce in schools and nurseries. One way to compensate for this, of course, is to encourage parents to provide these experiences at home, especially the practice and repetition in consolidating new skills that all children need but schools and nurseries cannot always find time for. The class teacher or staff co-ordinator should:

- ◆ explain the importance of spoken language for their children's progress at school;

- ◆ describe the sorts of things that parents can do to promote their children's spoken language generally, such as reciting nursery rhymes, singing simple songs, reading or telling stories, or simply talking to them about what they are doing while they are doing it. Many parents do not recognize the importance of these sorts of interaction with their children but are happy to provide it when it is pointed out to them;

- ◆ explain what the *One Step at a Time* programme is, what it is trying to achieve, and how parents can help their children learn the specific skills and vocabulary;

- ◆ provide opportunities for parents to work with their children, with staff guidance, either in the school or nursery or in after-hours workshops, so they can get a feel for how best to help them at home.

A school newsletter can keep parents up to date with what their children are learning month by month or term by term; home–school books can identify the specific skills or vocabulary that they are learning week by week. Parents can be encouraged to practise or reinforce these at home, by repeating and emphasizing the words of the week, focusing on specific conversation skills, practising nursery rhymes, playing 'I spy', etc.

Parents can help in the classroom in all sorts of ways, especially in the nursery and reception years, not necessarily by taking small groups or supporting individual children but by assisting in the simple daily routines of preparing for lessons and tidying away, putting on coats and boots and taking them off, or using knives and forks, pencils and scissors. This can free teaching staff to work with other children. Here too it will help if staff can find time to work with the parents first, explaining what needs to be done in the classroom, and showing them how to help, for example by talking with the children about what they are doing together. This will also help parents appreciate how they can support their own children at home.

The crucial first step, however, is to get parents interested and involved. Some will be only too happy to help at school or at home, but others may have decidedly mixed feelings about their own school experience and be reluctant to come further than the playground gate or the classroom door. Schools or nurseries may need to:

- ◆ issue personal invitations, followed by 'thank-you' letters;

- ◆ start with activities that are parent-friendly, such as accompanying their children on class outings, or even activities that are specifically for parents, like open sessions where a group of parents simply observe what goes on in the classroom, or a coffee morning, perhaps with cakes or biscuits that have been cooked in class by their children;

◆ select activities where it is easy for parents to get involved, such as art, craft and design, music and cookery, or looking at books or pictures with individual children;

◆ choose convenient times – the beginning of a morning or afternoon session seem most popular – and a suitable length of time, not too long at first;

◆ reassure parents about their involvement ('I won't have to read, will I?') and the likely cost of any visits or outings;

◆ take time to talk to them about the experience, what they have learned, and how they can use it to support their own children;

◆ and, above all, make sure they enjoy it and want to come back for more!

Implications for subsequent years

The development of spoken language does not end with Key Stage 1. It remains crucial to children's learning right through to further and higher education that they continue to extend their vocabulary and develop more complex and sophisticated ways of expressing themselves. So it is important that talk continues to be used in teaching and learning and in encouraging children to think for themselves. In particular, partner work (Chapter 12) and discussion work (Chapter 13) should remain standard classroom techniques in Key Stage 2 (children aged 7 to 11) and beyond. Indeed children who have been through the *One Step at a Time* programme will expect nothing less!

There is also much to be said for extending the *Discussion skills* programme over at least two years (Years 2 and 3 in England), though this may be difficult or impossible where children change schools between Year 2 and Year 3. Suitable topics will arise in all curriculum subjects, and teaching objectives through to Year 6 (children aged 10 to 11) can be found under Group Discussion and Interaction in *Speaking, Listening, Learning* (DfES, 2003).

In primary schools where children stay on until age 11, Key Stage 2 staff should be familiarized with the *One Step at a Time* programme that has been operating in Key Stage 1 and should be expected to build on it, particularly through the use of partner work, discussion work and curriculum vocabulary teaching. In some cases, Year 3 staff will need to continue the programme for children who have not completed all the checklists, or for the whole class if the programme has taken an extra year as discussed above. Either way, Year 2 staff will need to liaise with Year 3 staff and pass on details of children who have not completed checklists and the further support they may need.

It will be more difficult to provide this continuity where children leave an infant school at the end of Year 2 and enter a junior school. However, as well as passing on as much information about individual children as possible, infant school staff would do well to alert the junior school staff to the *One Step at a Time* strategy and how it has benefited their children including, once again, partner work, discussion work and curriculum vocabulary teaching.

9

Getting started

Getting started is a preliminary step of the programme for children who are not ready to begin the programme proper. This can be for different reasons: some children enter nursery very young or with limited experience; some are immature for their age; some are unfamiliar with English; some may have special needs which affect their spoken language either directly (for example specific language impairment, autism) or indirectly (for example hearing or visual impairments). Some of these children will catch up quickly and move into conversation fairly easily but others will not.

Children are not ready to begin *Conversation skills* until they are using combinations of two or more words most of the time. Most children are beginning to use a few words by the age of 18 months, and when they know between 20 and 50 words, usually around the age of 2, they will normally start putting them together in simple two or three word utterances. But some children are slow in acquiring these skills, and children who cannot easily form two-word combinations are clearly not ready for work on their conversation. They will need work on their pre-language skills instead.

Children need to develop the four Cs – *confidence*, *curiosity*, *concentration* and *communication* – before they will develop a fifth C: *conversation*. Confidence is perhaps the most important attribute that children need when they start their early education. Children need confidence to explore their environment, try new activities and relate to unfamiliar people. It comes initially from close, secure relationships with a few familiar adults.

Curiosity and concentration are developed primarily through play. By playing with adults, on their own, and eventually with other children, children learn about the things around them, acquire and practise new physical skills, and develop simple social skills like turn-taking, which later becomes a key element in conversation.

Communication also develops before children learn to speak. At least half of human communication is non-verbal, through posture and movement, gestures and facial expressions. Babies quickly learn to look to others for comfort and reassurance, and for information and guidance about what is happening. They are able to interpret other people's feelings and behaviour from facial expressions, posture and movement (body language), and soon learn how to communicate their own needs and wants by pointing and non-verbal sounds.

Getting started develops these pre-language skills, and establishes a basic vocabulary and the use of simple combinations of words. It differs from other steps in the programme in several respects.

- ◆ It is not necessarily a full year's programme – children can move to *Conversation skills* whenever they are ready.

- ◆ It does not have an initial screen – children who are identified as delayed on the *Conversation skills* screen should do *Getting started* instead.

- ◆ It has two skills checklists, not three, and they can be taught concurrently, not successively.

- ◆ Children at the *Getting started* stage need individual support as well as small-group work or whole-class teaching.

Children who have completed the *Getting started* step in the programme should be much better integrated into the life of the nursery or school. They will be more active, more engaged with and more interested in their physical surroundings, more confident in interacting with other people, and more able to initiate contact with both adults and other children. They will be able to communicate non-verbally through gestures, sounds and facial expressions, and they will also be beginning to communicate verbally, using simple combinations of words. They will be starting to play with dolls and toys, including constructional toys, on their own and with other children, and will be willing to join in other group activities, sharing and taking turns.

Initial screening

Getting started does not have its own initial screen. Instead, children identified as *Delayed* on the *Conversation skills* initial screen (Chapter 10), who do not have sufficient spoken language for systematic work on conversation, do *Getting started* instead. Initial screening is not always needed. Some schools or nurseries, especially in disadvantaged areas, may want to begin all their children on *Getting started*.

Initial screening is not always reliable at this age. Nursery children often lack confidence or experience of working with adults and other children, and as they gain confidence they may show increased engagement with their surroundings and increased responsiveness to other people, and become more talkative. The classification of children as *Competent*, *Developed* and *Delayed* should therefore be reconsidered at the start of the second term. However, children classified as *Delayed* on the *Conversation skills* initial screen, even provisionally, should begin with *Getting started* and not move on to *Conversation skills* until they can demonstrate the relevant skills.

Staff are sometimes surprised to discover how many of their children are delayed, and just how delayed some of them seem to be. If they would like a more detailed assessment of these children, not just in spoken language but also in their other areas of development,

Getting started

Conversation skills

Listening skills

Narrative skills

Discussion skills

they can use the Early Years Profile 3 from *Teaching Talking* (Locke and Beech, 2005). These are available separately from the rest of the *Teaching Talking* programme (see the section in Chapter 8 on children with special educational needs).

Children who are slow to speak, or whose speech is very unclear or jumbled, may have undiagnosed hearing problems. Ear infections such as 'glue ear' are very common at this age, and can have a serious effect on children's learning and social interaction. Staff should keep an eye out for tell-tale signs like a failure to understand or concentrate, especially in noisy situations, and should try a simple test like choosing a quiet time to talk softly behind a child's back to see if he notices. Children with hearing problems should, of course, be sat where they can clearly see the teacher, and also clearly see any other children who may be speaking.

Using the skills checklists (see Chapter 6)

Unlike the other steps in the programme, *Getting started* consists of just two checklists: *Learning through looking and listening* and *Learning through play*. They do not form a sequence and are intended to be used together, that is, staff can choose current teaching items from either or both checklists, depending on the needs of individual children.

The most critical are the skills listed under *Confidence* in the first checklist. Some children are withdrawn, passive or anxious when they first attend nursery, and it may take several weeks for them to play independently or relate to others. The best way to help them settle in is for each child to have one particular adult as their key worker or 'mother figure' who supports them in the daily domestic routines, plays with them wherever possible, and is their key emotional support while they get used to their new surroundings. Just helping these children acquire more confidence may be enough, and they may then demonstrate other skills that seemed to be missing. The activities in the *Listening* section have been found to be particularly useful in developing confidence in young children.

Procedure

❖ Staff should first observe children over a couple of weeks and note, for each child, any skills from the two checklists that are firmly established and any that are currently emerging or inconsistent. They can do this by, for example, putting a small dot in the tick box when a skill is first noticed, or using one tick for a skill that is emerging or inconsistent and two ticks for one that has been firmly established.

❖ Staff should then select two or three skills for current teaching, starting if possible with skills that are emerging or inconsistent. In classes where most or all children are on the programme staff have found it useful to identify just one or two skills at a time, and make them an objective for all children and all staff for a couple of weeks. This is simpler and clearer for support staff, and helps ensure that everyone focuses on those particular skills with all children across the day.

❖ A list of the skills selected for current teaching should be displayed prominently in the classroom so all staff can refer to them and encourage and reinforce them whenever they are working with children from that group.

Getting started

Conversation skills   Listening skills   Narrative skills   Discussion skills

Classroom intervention (see Chapter 6)

It is accepted nursery practice for each child to have a designated member of staff with special responsibility for seeing them through the daily domestic routines. These family groupings can also be the basis of *Getting started* intervention. The key-worker or person in charge of each group is best placed to provide the close personal interaction that these children need.

Procedure

❖ The key-worker should ensure that all children in her group have at least 10–15 minutes every day, not necessarily all at once, working on the skills that they are currently learning. This can be during whole-class activities, group work, free activity sessions or daily classroom routines.

❖ Whole-class activities and group work can be used for the *Learning through looking and listening* checklist but may not be immediately appropriate for *Learning through play*. Staff should instead make opportunities in free activity sessions to play with each child on their own or with other children, depending on the type of play being developed.

Teaching method

The key factors in developing early communication skills (see Chapter 3) are:

◆ adult–child interaction

◆ physical involvement

◆ active encouragement

◆ repetition, repetition, repetition.

These are most easily provided where there is a good ratio of adults to children, as there usually is at home. They can be more difficult to provide in schools and nurseries, but opportunities can be found or created that are just as natural, spontaneous and valuable.

The following are the key teaching techniques (see Chapter 6).

◆ *Modelling*: the adult demonstrates the skill she wants children to learn, for example she shows an interest or gets involved in what other children are doing, and encourages the child to do likewise. Imitation is a powerful means of teaching and learning.

◆ *Highlighting*: the adult draws attention to the relevant skill by pointing it out and emphasizing whenever it occurs: 'Look how Johnny is marching to the music!' or 'Jill is playing with Jenny. That looks fun!'

◆ *Prompting*: the adult encourages the child to respond, directing him towards the appropriate behaviour, for example 'Now you do it too' or 'Can Sam play with you?'

◆ *Rewarding*: the adult rewards appropriate responses with praise and further encouragement. If the praise can emphasize what was good about the response – 'That was good, when you copied me' or 'Thank you for pointing. Now I know what you want' – it will help children to recognize what it is that you want them to learn. If a response is not quite what the adult is looking for, she can encourage a more appropriate response by asking questions, prompting or modelling the skill again.

At this early stage, as well as modelling relevant behaviour themselves for the children to copy, staff are likely to use children's behaviour as a model for their own intervention. For example, the child points at something so the adult points at it too, says what it is, and talks about it. This is a particularly effective method of highlighting behaviours with young children.

Almost any nursery activity can be used for teaching these skills. Specific materials are not needed. The daily routines of entering or leaving the nursery, dressing and undressing, eating and drinking, preparation and tidying up, and toileting and washing, provide valuable opportunities for modelling, encouraging and rewarding skills like looking, listening and turn-taking. Teacher-led activities like cooking, PE, music, nursery rhymes or story-time can be used to model, practise and reinforce skills like copying an adult or taking part in a group activity. Circle-time can be used to practise skills like turn-taking or locating a sound or the person who is talking. Free activity sessions provide opportunities for encouraging all these skills and promoting all types of play.

It is important to repeat the same activities many times. Young children do not normally understand a new activity until they have experienced it a number of times, so they should be repeated for at least a couple of weeks. Nursery staff sometimes think that they need to keep changing the content of lessons, to retain children's interest and extend their experience. Children under the age of 5 will always benefit from repeating the same activities again and again, particularly if they are having difficulty with spoken language.

It is also important to ensure that these activities involve and include all children. By the end of the day staff may feel that they have never stopped, but videos of nursery activity show that while some children are involved in many activities, others hardly join in at all. This is why it is important that each child has a designated member of staff who makes a point of attending specifically to that child every day, to model, elicit and/or reward one or more of the targeted behaviours.

Vocabulary teaching (see Chapter 7)

Vocabulary teaching is particularly important with *Getting started* children as a way of developing the two-word combinations that they need to use if they are to be ready for *Conversation skills*. It is difficult to teach young children grammatical forms as such, so *Getting started* concentrates instead on teaching elementary nouns and verbs and a few other words. Once children know a range of different words, including words of different types, they will normally start putting them together for themselves – *more drink, big ball* – but some children may need to be taught more words, or more words of different types, before they begin to combine them. Others may need to be shown how to put them together.

Getting started

Conversation skills

Listening skills

Narrative skills

Discussion skills

Most children know at least 100 words by the age of 3 so the *Starter vocabulary* (adapted from Locke, 1985) consists of the 100 words that children seem most likely to learn first. These words are, of course, very simple but easily taken for granted, and staff have found it useful to have them listed so that they can check which words their children are actually using. They can be varied if other words are likely to be more familiar or more appropriate, for example *trainers* instead of *shoes*, *pants* instead of *trousers*, *water* instead of *juice*. Some variants, for example *cat/pussy*, are given already.

Early vocabulary should be taught through simple conversation based around what the child is doing. Staff should listen carefully to what the child is saying and simplify their own language to the same level, while using it to introduce new words. For example, if a child says 'hot' or 'more', the adult can reply, 'Yes, your dinner is hot' or 'Do you want some more drink?' This helps familiarize children both with new vocabulary and also with simple word combinations. But children should not be pressured into putting new words together as that is likely to be counter-productive.

Young children find it easiest to learn vocabulary by being actively involved with familiar objects including toys. So nouns like *spoon* or *dinner* should be taught when the child is eating; verbs like *run* and *jump* during PE; adjectives like *wet* or *dirty* when the child is washing or drying his hands; and prepositions like *in* or *on* by getting children to climb into a box or on to a chair. Physical activity seems particularly important in grasping spatial concepts. The more abstract verbs like *give* or *want* are also best taught by referring to what a child is actually doing. Once children are beginning to use a word, staff can use less familiar contexts, and pictures as well as real objects, to extend and consolidate learning.

Procedure

❖ The staff member in charge of each group should select four to six words from the *Starter vocabulary* for teaching to the children in her group. They should normally be a mixture of nouns and verbs, for example four nouns and two verbs, with the other words added later on.

❖ She should start with any words that some children in the group are already using. When all the children in the group know that word she can select another, and so on through the list. Since the aim at this level is to develop children's use of two-word utterances, it is important that they are actually using the words in question.

❖ In addition to skills teaching, all children should have at least 10–15 minutes every day, not necessarily all at once, working on current vocabulary. This can be during whole-class activities, group work, free activity sessions or daily classroom routines. Vocabulary teaching should be combined with other activities wherever possible.

❖ The words identified for current teaching should be displayed prominently so staff can refer to them and model and encourage those words whenever they are working with children from that group. The words that they need to learn can be entered on a *Vocabulary checklist* (Appendix 2) and ticked off as each child learns them.

Getting started

Conversation skills

Listening skills

Narrative skills

Discussion skills

Procedure

❖ If all or most children in the class are on the *Getting started* programme, it may be useful to identify the same words for teaching to all children in the class. This is simpler and clearer for support staff, and helps to ensure that everyone focuses on those particular words with all children across the day.

❖ Teaching a particular word should normally continue until all children in the group have learned it. This may take several weeks. It does not matter if children are learning at different rates – all children will benefit from the extra practice – but if one or two children are having particular difficulty they should not delay the rest. They will need whatever additional support the school can provide.

The best way to assess and monitor children's vocabulary is through one-to-one conversation. Because this is difficult and time-consuming in large classes, staff at the other steps of the programme are advised to concentrate on children's understanding of the relevant vocabulary. But with *Getting started* it is important that children are actually using the words, not just understanding them.

Staff may find it useful to build up a stock of material illustrating the *Starter vocabulary*, including pictures from shopping catalogues (especially children's catalogues), computer Clip Art and/or photographs, especially photos of the children themselves, as well as commercial products like the LDA *Chatterbox*. Pictures should not be used when introducing new words but can be used for consolidation and for checking understanding.

Reviewing progress and moving on (see Chapter 6)

Children may move from *Getting started* to *Conversation skills* at any time during the year. The sooner they do this, the more progress they will make on *Conversation skills* before going up to Reception. But it is important not to do this too quickly as these children will need as much practice and consolidation in basic skills as they can get.

Procedure

❖ Staff can keep a running record of individual progress by entering children's names on a checklist and ticking off each skill or word as the child acquires it. A skill should not be credited unless the child is using it *confidently*, *competently* and *consistently*.

❖ Staff should also review all children at the end of term or the beginning of the next term, to bring records up to date and consider whether they are ready to move to *Conversation skills*.

❖ Children should not move to *Conversation skills* unless they would qualify as *Developing* on the *Conversation skills* initial screen, that is, they show all the behaviours in Band 1 and at least one behaviour from Band 2 (see Chapter 10).

Getting started

Procedure

❖ The most critical of these behaviours is that they are combining two or more words most of the time. Staff can use this as an indication of whether children are ready for assessment or reassessment on the *Conversation skills* initial screen. Once children are combining two or more words in most of their talk staff can assess whether they demonstrate the other behaviours, namely:

  – they communicate verbally or non-verbally with other children *and* will talk to adults if encouraged (Band 1), and

  – they *either* follow simple instructions, respond verbally to questions or comments, *or* will talk spontaneously to adults or other children (Band 2).

Children who move from *Getting started* to *Conversation skills* may not be able to complete the *Conversation skills* programme by the end of the nursery year, and there may even be some children who are still not ready to begin *Conversation skills*. See the section in Chapter 8 on children from *Getting started* who do not complete *Conversation skills* by the end of the year.

Getting started

Learning through looking and listening

Getting started

Checklist 1

Child's name

Confidence

| Responds to smiles, and will make eye contact |
| Will initiate contact with a familiar adult |
| Will seek affection, comfort, etc. from a familiar adult |
| Responds to adult approval and encouragement |

Looking

| Shows interest in their surroundings |
| Responds appropriately to pointing |
| Copies adults or other children |
| Examines unfamiliar objects or toys |
| Will look at pictures with an adult |
| Will follow a picture book with an adult |

Listening

| Can recognize some things by their sound |
| Is responsive to person talking when in a group |
| Joins in action games and songs |
| Can locate sounds or person talking |
| Can march or clap in time to familiar music |

Communication

| Shows interest in other children |
| Interacts with other children |
| Will join in group activities led by an adult |
| Responds to facial expressions |
| Communicates by pointing or facial expressions |
| Communicates vocally with adults and other children |
| Can give at least one-word response to questions |

Getting started   Conversation skills   Listening skills   Narrative skills   Discussion skills

Getting started

Learning through play

Getting started

Conversation skills Listening skills Narrative skills Discussion skills

Child's name

Solo play

| Solitary play with materials, objects, toys, etc. |
| Parallel play (alongside but not with other children) |

Taking turns

| Understands simple turn-taking activities like passing a ball backwards and forwards |
| Will wait for turn in familiar activities and routines |
| Will wait for turn in unfamiliar activities |

Playing with others

| Simple informal games with adults, for example hiding and finding things |
| Imitative play (copying adults or other children) |
| Informal games with other children, for example chasing and hiding |
| Will help other children if asked |
| Will include other children in play |
| Will share toys etc. with other children |
| Co-operative play with other children (taking turns or sharing) |

Imaginative play

| Simple play with musical instruments, art materials, etc. |
| Constructive play with sand, dough, bricks, etc. |
| Creative play (simple art and craft work) |
| Simple pretend play with dolls, toys, etc. |

Checklist 2

Starter vocabulary

Nouns			Verbs			Other words	
baby	ball	apple	brush	come		big	
daddy	bike	biscuit	clap	find		dirty	
man	bricks	dinner	cook	get		hot	
mummy	bus	plate	cry	give		wet	
	car	spoon	cut	like/love			
eyes	doll	sweets	drink	look (at)		down	
feet	duck		dry	make		in	
hair	pram	cup	eat	play		on	
hands	swing	drink	hit	put		up	
mouth	teddy/bear	milk	jump	want			
nose		orange/juice	kick			gone	
toes	book	water	push			more	
tummy/belly	box		read				
	paper	bed	run			yes	
bag	pencil	chair	sit			no	
dress		house	sleep				
hat	bird	table	stand				
jacket	cat/pussy		throw				
pants/knickers	dog	brush	walk				
shoes	flower	soap	wash				
socks	tree	tap					
trousers		towel					

One Step at a Time © Ann Locke (Network Continuum Education, 2006)

Discussion skills Narrative skills Listening skills Conversation skills Getting started

Getting started

Conversation skills

Listening skills

Narrative skills

Discussion skills

Notes on Checklist 1:
Learning through looking and listening

This checklist develops children's confidence and the basic pre-verbal skills of looking, listening and non-verbal communication.

Confidence

Confidence is perhaps the most important attribute that children need when they start their early education. It can take them several weeks to gain the confidence that they need to explore their environment, try new activities or relate to others in the nursery. They need a warm and trusting relationship with one or more adults, and a secure and protective environment where they can relate easily to adults and each other. Staff can then build their confidence through physical contact, talking to them, showing approval and highlighting successes, and promoting friendships with other children. Giving and rewarding simple responsibilities, such as taking something to another child or getting something from another teacher, are also good ways of building children's confidence.

Most children will show the skills in this part of the checklist once they feel secure with an adult or other children. Staff can promote particular responses by doing things with them, giving them things to play with, and rewarding any response with smiles and encouragement.

Looking

Children learn a great deal both from looking at their surroundings and from looking at other people but may lack the confidence to do this in unfamiliar situations or with unfamiliar adults. They may need to be encouraged to explore and handle things for themselves, and to respond when adults point things out to them.

Children who have learned to look to others for reassurance and guidance will begin to copy the behaviour and reactions they observe. Copying may have to be one-to-one (teacher–child) at first, before including children in group activities like 'Simon says', 'Follow my leader' or 'This is the way we wash our hands'. At this stage, looking at pictures or picture books may also need to be one-to-one, so that the adult can be sure that the child understands or recognizes what is happening.

Listening

Listening is important, not just for learning to talk but for understanding most of what goes on in the classroom or nursery. If children are slow to respond to speech, staff need to be sure that they can hear what is being said, and make appropriate arrangements if they are having any difficulty. But there is more to listening than just hearing. Children also need to be able to recognize different sounds, including the sounds of the human voice, and to appreciate their significance, including the special significance of talk as a means of communication.

Most children should be able to recognize familiar sounds like the classroom bell, musical toys, sirens, birds singing or dogs barking. This can be taught and tested using simple games like 'What made that noise?' But many children will find listening in a group more difficult than listening one-to-one. They may not even realize that an adult is talking to them, and staff may have to get their attention by naming them individually: 'Are you listening, Jason?' Action games and songs like 'Miss Polly had a dolly' or 'The wheels on the bus' will also help children to listen in a group. Location of sounds can be taught and tested using circle games, for example a child sits in the middle of the circle with their eyes closed, and the other children take it in turns to call out, ring a bell or bang a drum.

Communication

Helping children to develop good non-verbal communication skills is crucial for the emergence of spoken language. This includes looking, smiling and other facial expressions, touches and gestures, and shared activity. Some children may need to be helped to engage with other children, and then to respond to them.

Staff should look for opportunities where they can demonstrate facial expressions or simple physical gestures like pointing out things of interest, shrugging their shoulders or clapping their hands to show they are pleased. Children may also need to be taught non-verbal vocal communication such as making pleased noises, laughing or shouting to indicate something or attract someone's attention. The simplest form of verbal communication is to indicate wants and needs by naming things, for example *drink*! … *biscuit*!

Getting started

Conversation skills

Listening skills

Narrative skills

Discussion skills

Notes on Checklist 2:
Learning through play

This checklist uses children's play as a means of developing confidence, curiosity, concentration and communication. Play is one of the most important ways in which children learn about the world around them and about other people. It:

- ◆ teaches children how to explore the physical world;

- ◆ enables children to practise the basic physical skills of handling materials, using tools, etc.;

- ◆ helps them to discover their abilities, and what they like and dislike doing;

- ◆ teaches them how to interact with adults and get on with other children;

- ◆ encourages simple communication with adults and other children, and provides practice in talk;

- ◆ gives children something to talk about and reasons to communicate, for example to get help or co-ordinate behaviour;

- ◆ trains them in taking turns, which is a crucial skill when children come to conversation.

Children who seem to be just playing may be learning much more than they will ever learn from any lesson. The extent to which they talk while playing, to themselves or to others, is also a good measure of their communication skills. Children who are slow in acquiring communication skills may need more play, over a longer period, than other children. Children who play silently need to be encouraged to talk about what they are doing.

Children's play takes different forms and develops through a series of stages, as shown in the table on page 84. The teacher should take time to observe each child in their spontaneous play to get some idea of their current development and the skills they currently have or lack. Some children will move easily from one type of play to another as they gain more experience and more confidence in the different sorts of play. Others may need to be encouraged and rewarded more explicitly, with the teacher carefully introducing them to new activities or situations, and showing them how to play by playing with them.

Turn-taking is particularly important, both as a social behaviour and as preparation for the to-and-fro of conversation. Children may need to learn both how to take their turn and how to take both roles, for example passing an object and taking it back again, and, eventually, first speaking and then listening. They may learn how to wait their turn in familiar classroom routines but still find it difficult to wait in an exciting new activity, such as stirring the cooking mixture or playing with a new piece of equipment. Staff may have to model and encourage these behaviours.

Play with other children should not be hurried. Children who are still at the stages of solitary or parallel play can be encouraged to watch other children playing and to tolerate their presence during their own play but they should not be made to play with them if they are not ready. Friendships can be encouraged by grouping children who have similar

Getting started

Conversation skills

Listening skills

Narrative skills

Discussion skills

abilities and interests and are likely to be friendly without being dominating or over-protective. Some children will also need to be encouraged to involve themselves in activities such as playing with equipment and large toys (riding, pulling, pushing, etc.), physical play (rough and tumble), or creative and pretend play.

Staff can encourage the different types of play by:

◆ providing frequent opportunities and the appropriate materials;

◆ playing with the children at their current level of development and involving other children and adults as appropriate;

◆ modelling, prompting and rewarding the relevant behaviours and skills, for example persistence, co-operation and turn-taking: 'You played with that bus for such a long time' … 'Wasn't it nice playing with Paul?' … 'Thank you for letting Susan have a turn';

◆ ensuring that children engage in a range of play activities and don't spend all their time in just one type of play.

Getting started

Conversation skills

Listening skills

Narrative skills

Discussion skills

Getting started

Conversation skills   Listening skills   Narrative skills   Discussion skills

The development of play

	Physical play	Constructional play	Table-top play	Imaginative play
Birth to about 2 years **Early experience and exploration:** children explore their physical environment through all the senses, developing curiosity **Social interaction:** *Solitary play:* children play on their own but may like a familiar adult nearby *Parallel play:* children play alongside but not with other children	Rough and tumble with adults Water play, for example paddling, splashing Play with sand Push-and-pull and sit-and-ride toys, for example toy cars, bikes, etc.	Play with activity centres, blocks, bricks, play dough, clay, modelling clay, etc. Making mud pies, sand castles, dough cakes, etc. Play with stacking or nesting boxes or beakers, posting boxes, insert boards, etc.	Cutting and pasting Painting, colouring, drawing using crayons, pencils, finger paints, etc.	Play with musical objects and instruments (rattles, shakers, drums, etc.) Hiding and finding Play with household objects (brushes, saucepans, etc.) Pretend play with dolls, toys, shoes, hats, bags, cardboard boxes
About 2 to 4 years **Learning from others:** children's understanding and use of talk is increased through shared activities with adults and children **Social interaction:** *Imitative play:* children copy adult activities and behaviour, or the play of other children *Co-operative play:* children begin to recognize and conform to the norms of social behaviour and co-operative activities	Climbing, jumping, balancing Swings and slides Kicking, throwing, catching bean-bags, balls, etc. Rough and tumble with other children, for example chasing, hiding	Building walls, towers, making models with bricks, blocks, etc. Large-piece jigsaw puzzles	Work with scissors, crayons, paintbrushes, glue, etc. to produce pictures, cards, collages, friezes, etc. Small-piece jigsaw puzzles	Dressing up Copying adults ('helping' to cook, sweep, mend the car, etc.) Pretend social routines (cooking, cleaning, driving a bus, going to bed, etc.) Pretend social settings (playing houses, shops, doctor/dentist, post office, etc.)
From about 4 years **Learning with others:** children use their experience and imagination to join in and make up free and rule-governed activities **Social interaction:** *Rule-governed play:* children understand and take part in activities involving rules	Rule-governed games like 'hide and seek', 'kiss chase', 'statue', 'tig', 'British bulldog', etc. Races, obstacle courses, team games	Making models, with and without instruction, with and without guidance, and with and without other children	Free and directed art and design work, with and without adult help Board and card games	Using props to act out real-life situations Fantasy games with other children

10

Conversation skills

Getting started

Conversation skills

Listening skills

Narrative skills

Discussion skills

Conversation is the most basic of all language skills. It is through conversation that we learn to speak in the first place. Parents talk to their babies almost from birth, and babies respond at an astonishingly early age, at first with interest and facial expressions, then with noises and baby sounds. These mock conversations, with parents talking to their babies and the babies 'talking' back, are the foundation of spoken language. By the age of 2 or 3 most children are enthusiastic conversationalists, eager to talk with familiar adults and sometimes difficult to stop. But children who have not had the same encouragement to talk with their parents may have restricted conversational skills even at 4 or 5.

Conversation is also a basic social skill. It is through conversation that we learn to relate to other people, both adults and children. We use conversation to make initial contact, maintain friendships, co-ordinate our actions and resolve disagreements. Without conversation children will be isolated and limited in their ability to influence what is going on around them.

Conversation is also the basis of most learning and teaching especially, but not only, in the early years. We use conversation to teach young children about the world around them, by talking with them about what they are doing or things that have attracted their attention, and we use their replies to gauge what they know and what they still need to learn. We also use conversation to teach spoken language itself.

Conversation is not just an essential language skill that children need to acquire; it is a skill they need to learn in order to acquire other language skills. We teach both vocabulary and grammar through conversation, by building on what children are saying and adding new words or more structure: 'Ball!' 'Yes, that's a ball. Isn't it a *big* ball!' We also use conversation to monitor children's understanding, to pick up on things that they seem not to have grasped or to ask them questions. Conversation introduces children by easy stages to the idea of a sequence of sentences, and hence to the idea of an account, an explanation or a narrative.

Conversation is more than just talk. To hold a conversation children need a basic vocabulary; they need to be able to join words together to form sentences; they need to be able to identify and comment on things around them; and they need to be able to answer questions and, if necessary, ask them. But they also need a number of other social and linguistic skills (sometimes called 'conversational etiquette') such as knowing how to make contact with other people and initiate a conversation with them; how to take turns as speaker and as listener; how to follow and keep to a topic; and how to recognize that others have not understood, and know how to repair the failure.

Children also need to be familiar with the many different uses of conversation, for example commenting, directing, asking, expressing their feelings, needs and wants, and negotiating or agreeing plans and behaviour, and with the many different contexts in which conversation can occur. It is important to ensure that their conversation skills are not limited to particular topics or situations – and in particular not restricted to small-group teaching sessions! We should not assume that because children can demonstrate a skill in small-group or one-to-one work, they will use it spontaneously in other contexts.

Most children can hold some sort of a conversation by the time they start school or nursery, but some cannot. These children will be significantly disadvantaged in what they can do and in what they can learn. Many other children will still be developing their conversation skills. Some nursery-year children do not have sufficient spoken language for systematic work on conversation. These children should work through the preliminary step in the programme, *Getting started*, instead. The *Conversation skills* initial screen identifies children for whom *Getting started* is the appropriate programme, but some schools or nurseries in disadvantaged areas may want to begin all their children on *Getting started*.

Children who have completed the *Conversation skills* step in the programme should be much more confident, both socially and linguistically. They will be willing to talk with different people about different things, in different situations and during different activities, about what they have done and things that have happened, both inside and outside school. They will understand and use significantly more complex sentences. They will be able to learn about the world through talk as well as through physical contact and play, and be starting to explain and predict things as well as to describe them.

Initial screening (see Chapter 6)

> **Procedure**
>
> ❖ Once children have settled into their new class staff should spend at least a week observing their spoken language in a variety of situations, both formal and informal, and focusing on the skills that are to be assessed.
>
> ❖ They should then complete the initial screen for all the children in their class or group. This should be done in discussion with colleagues, in pairs or threes or at a staff meeting.
>
> ❖ Each screen is divided into three bands and children are assessed band by band. This means that if children do not have all the skills in Band 1, they do not need to be assessed on Band 2; and if they do not have all the skills in Band 2, they do not need to be assessed on Band 3.

Procedure

❖ A skill should be credited only if a child is using it *confidently*, *competently* and *consistently*. If there is any doubt or disagreement, or the child's use of the particular skill is irregular or infrequent, it should not be credited. At this stage it is better to underestimate children's abilities than overestimate them.

❖ Children who have all the skills in Bands 1 and 2 and at least one skill in Band 3 are identified as reasonably *Competent* in the relevant skills.

❖ Children who have all the skills in Band 1 and at least one skill in Band 2 are identified as *Developing* the relevant skills.

❖ All other children, that is, children who do not have all the skills in Band 1 and at least one skill in Band 2, are identified as *Delayed* in the relevant skills.

Note that children who do not have all the skills in Band 1 count as *Delayed* even if they have more than one skill in Band 2; and children who do not have all the skills in Band 2 still count as *Developing* even if they have more than one skill in Band 3.

Children identified as *Delayed* are not ready for systematic work on their conversation skills and should work on *Getting started* instead (see Chapter 9). Some of these children will improve and move up to *Conversation skills* quickly but others will not. Staff are sometimes surprised to discover how many of their children are delayed, and just how delayed some of them seem to be. If they would like a more detailed assessment of these children, not just in spoken language but also in their other areas of development, they can use the Early Years Profile 3 from *Teaching Talking* (Locke and Beech, 2005). These are available separately from the rest of the *Teaching Talking* programme (see also the section in Chapter 8 on children with special educational needs).

Initial screening is not always reliable at this age. Nursery children often lack confidence or experience of working with adults and other children, and as they gain confidence they may show increased engagement with their surroundings, increased responsiveness to other people and become more talkative. The classification of children as *Competent*, *Developed* and *Delayed* should therefore be reconsidered at the start of the second term. But children classified as *Delayed* on the *Conversation skills* initial screen, even provisionally, should begin with *Getting started* and not move on to *Conversation skills* until they can demonstrate the relevant skills.

Children who are slow to speak, or whose speech is very unclear or jumbled, may have undiagnosed hearing problems. Ear infections such as 'glue ear' are very common at this age, and can have a serious effect on children's learning and social interaction. Staff should keep an eye out for tell-tale signs like a failure to understand or concentrate, especially in noisy situations, and try a simple test like choosing a quiet time to talk softly behind a child's back and see if he notices.

Using the skills checklists (see Chapter 6)

There are three checklists: *Early conversation skills*, *Basic conversation skills* and *Further conversation skills*. As their names suggest, they are really one long checklist, divided into term-sized chunks. They include conversational contexts and conversational uses as well as conversational skills.

Procedure

❖ Staff should work through each checklist in turn, focusing on just a few items at a time. Each skill should be made an explicit teaching objective for one or more weeks to ensure that all staff focus on that skill with all children and in all relevant activities, across the day and through the week.

❖ This can be a rolling programme of three or four skills at a time. This means that the class starts with one or two skills in the first week, adds another one or two in the second week, then replaces one or two with new skills in the third week, and so on.

❖ The sequence of skills in the checklist is meant only as a guide. Intervention should also be guided by the skills that children are developing spontaneously. In teaching one skill, staff will often have been introducing another, and this can provide an easy transition from one skill to the next.

❖ Staff may find it helpful to identify in advance the skills they are going to teach and the order in which they are going to teach them, and build them into their advance planning, so lessons can be prepared, resources gathered and support staff guided in their work with small groups or individual children. However, planning needs to be flexible because some skills may take longer to learn than expected, and some weeks should be left free so that staff can go back and repeat or reinforce any skills that children have been finding difficult.

❖ A list of the skills selected for current teaching should be displayed prominently in the classroom so all staff can refer to them and encourage and reinforce them at all times during the day.

Classroom intervention (see Chapter 6)

Procedure

❖ Each skill should be introduced, explained and/or demonstrated to the class or group as a whole before being made the focus of small-group work. When introducing any new skill or activity it is always good practice to explain what it is that children need to learn, and why they need to learn it. If children know what is expected of them they are much more likely to exhibit the behaviour in question.

❖ There should then be at least one whole-class activity every day focusing on the skills currently being learned. These need not be separate or special lessons – they can be curriculum lessons, circle-time or story-time, activities like art and design, PE or music – but staff should identify at least one specific occasion each day when an adult will model, encourage and reinforce the relevant skills for all children, not just for those receiving small-group work.

❖ All staff should be encouraged to use every other opportunity through the day, including playtime and dinnertime, to model, encourage and reinforce these skills with individual children.

Getting started | Conversation skills | Listening skills | Narrative skills | Discussion skills

Procedure

❖ Staff should also try to ensure that every child has at least one conversation, or attempt at conversation, with an adult every day. It is good nursery practice for each child to have a designated member of staff with special responsibility for seeing them through the daily domestic routines. It should be this person's responsibility to have at least one extended conversation with each child in her care every day.

Small-group work

❖ Each group should be of four to six children. As far as possible, each group should always be led by the same member of staff.

❖ Children identified as *Developing* (including children who have moved up from *Getting started*) should be given 10–15 minutes small-group conversation work every day if possible, certainly two or three times a week. Children identified as *Competent* should be given 10–15 minutes small-group language work at least once a week.

❖ It is usually convenient to group the children identified as *Developing*, and the children identified as *Competent*, because that is easier to schedule and makes it easier to support and monitor the children most in need of it. But children will also benefit from mixed-ability groupings. Absences can give opportunities to include *Competent* children in the *Developing* groups.

❖ The same groupings can be used as for other purposes but language teaching should be additional to other small-group work. Groups can be reorganized if children progress at different rates through the year.

❖ Small-group teaching should proceed at a pace that includes every child. It is better to consolidate a skill for all children than to push ahead too quickly. It does not matter if children are learning at different rates; all children will benefit from the extra practice. However, if some children are still learning a skill after three or more weeks, it may be sensible to leave it for a while and come back to it again later.

❖ Teaching a particular skill should normally continue until all the children in that group have learned it, but if one or two children are having particular difficulty they should not delay the rest. They will need whatever additional support staff can provide. If several children in the class are having difficulty it may be necessary to continue teaching that skill to these children, and possibly the whole class, for longer than originally planned.

Teaching method

Most children are capable of holding extended conversations by the time they are 3, and by the age of 4 the main preoccupation of many teachers and parents will be to find ways of stopping them talking! Nevertheless, all nursery-age children have much to learn about conversation and will benefit from extensive practice. Some will need systematic teaching to help them establish and consolidate the necessary skills.

Some children will get lots of conversational experience and encouragement at home while others may get very little. It is important to give these latter children as much opportunity and personal encouragement as possible. All staff – not just teachers and classroom assistants but dinner ladies, playground assistants and site staff – should do all they can to involve every child in conversation about anything that is going on at any time in the nursery. Talking with – not at, not to, but with – children should be part of everyone's job description!

The key factors in developing early communication skills (see Chapter 3) are:

◆ adult–child interaction

◆ physical involvement

◆ active encouragement

◆ repetition, repetition, repetition.

These are most easily provided where there is a good ratio of adults to children, as there usually is at home. They can be more difficult to provide in schools and nurseries, but opportunities for developing conversation can be found or created that are just as natural, spontaneous and valuable.

Conversation skills can be taught using any activity and any resource – anything that captures children's interest and encourages them to talk about it. Teacher-led activities such as playground games, art and design, cooking, PE, music and nursery rhymes can be used to model, practise and reinforce specific skills, such as responding, directing and turn-taking. None of these requires special resources or materials. The daily routines of entering and leaving the nursery, dressing and undressing, eating and drinking, preparation and tidying up, and toileting and washing also provide valuable opportunities for talking with children about what they are doing. Children may sometimes think that they are supposed to be silent during these activities; staff may need to make it clear that they are allowed to talk.

Almost any nursery activity can be used for teaching conversation skills, but two activities are particularly useful:

◆ *talk-time*, where children sit with their key-worker to talk about things that have happened or will happen, what they have done, the people they will meet and so on, including their behaviour and feelings. All children should have a talk-time session of around 10 minutes, in small or larger groups, every day;

◆ *circle games*, where children practise a specific skill one after another, going round the circle. For example, they take it in turns to smile and say 'Hello' to the child next to them or the teacher puts a pile of toys in the middle of the circle and the children take turns to ask the next child to fetch them one. Circle games can be used in small-group teaching with five or six children and reinforced by playing the same games in larger groups of 10–15 children in normal classroom circle-time.

In addition, daily routines are particularly suited for teaching social contact, expressing feelings, needs and wants, and commenting and directing; informal activities are particularly suited for teaching turn-taking, maintaining conversation and negotiation; structured activities are particularly suited for teaching listening and responding, clarification and repair. But conversation skills can be practised in any context, and the teaching of a particular skill should not be restricted to any one activity or type of activity. The following are the key teaching techniques (see Chapter 6).

◆ *Modelling*: the adult demonstrates the skill she wants children to learn, for example she greets each child in turn, or shows that she is listening attentively as a child speaks to her. Imitation is a powerful means of teaching and learning.

◆ *Highlighting*: the adult draws attention to the relevant skill by discussing it, emphasizing its importance or explaining when or why we use it, for example when we should ask for help or permission or why we should look at someone when they are speaking to us. She can do this by asking questions – 'What do we say when someone comes to visit us?' … 'What can you do when you don't understand something?' – discussing the children's responses, and then summarizing and highlighting the key points: 'So what do we do when someone comes into our classroom? We look at them, we smile and we say "Hello".'

◆ *Prompting*: the adult encourages the child to respond, directing him towards the appropriate behaviour: 'Can you tell me some more about that?' … 'Can I help you? What would you like me to do?' … 'Did you want to ask me about that?'

◆ *Rewarding*: the adult rewards appropriate responses with praise and further encouragement. If the praise can emphasise what was good about the response – 'Thank you for listening to me.' … 'We had a good talk together, didn't we?' … 'Ah! Now I understand.' – it will help children recognize what it is you want them to learn. If a response is not quite what the adult is looking for, she can encourage a more appropriate response by asking questions, prompting or modelling the skill again.

If children are having particular difficulty acquiring conversation skills, staff should:

◆ make time to talk with them individually about what they are doing, several times a day;

◆ provide additional daily talk-time in groups of no more than six, fewer if possible, not just to focus on specific skills but also to encourage and reward any form of talk;

◆ ensure that other staff are aware of the skills currently being taught, so that they can model, elicit and reward them wherever appropriate;

◆ discuss these children with their parents or carers, and get their involvement if possible.

Vocabulary teaching (see Chapter 7)

The *Conversation skills* vocabulary consists mostly of adjectives and prepositions, with some basic curriculum nouns. Children will find these words more difficult to grasp than the concrete nouns and verbs of their early vocabulary, but they will learn them, too, through practical involvement with real objects. This is particularly important with prepositions: children learn *in* and *on, behind* and *in front*, by putting things – or, even better, themselves – inside or on top of, behind or in front of something. Quantity terms can also be taught through practical activities, for example pulling off *a bit* of modelling clay or getting *another* book off the shelf. Adjectives should also be introduced and explained using concrete examples (a *big* teddy, a *heavy* box) that children can handle for themselves, and the nouns can be taught by doing or making things (cutting out a *square*, playing with a *clock*, acting out what happens at *night*, celebrating a *birthday*).

Getting started

Conversation skills

Listening skills

Narrative skills

Discussion skills

Procedure

❖ Staff should identify 6–10 words for teaching each week as 'this week's special words'. As well as words chosen from current curriculum topics, they should include between two and four words from the *Conversation skills* vocabulary list. If children are finding some words difficult they can be featured over several weeks, or repeated at different times during the year.

❖ It will usually be convenient to teach a selection of words from the same category (quality, colour, etc.) at the same time, but staff should avoid words that are similar in sound or meaning (for example *big* and *biggest*, *loud* and *noisy*) and contrasting pairs (for example *dry* and *wet*, *quick* and *slow*), which some children will find confusing.

❖ The words for the week should be introduced and explained to the whole class at the beginning of the week, and displayed prominently in the classroom for reference by children as well as staff.

❖ These words should then be included and featured by all staff on every possible occasion over the rest of the week, in whole-class lessons, group work, one-to-one interaction and classroom routines.

❖ Towards the end of the week staff should monitor the learning of all children and identify any words that seem to be proving particularly difficult. Children who are slow in acquiring new vocabulary should be checked individually.

❖ The crucial test is that these children understand the word in question, whether or not they are using it (they may be copying other children). Understanding can be checked by asking questions, or giving instructions and seeing if children respond appropriately, while making sure they are not following other children.

❖ Any children who have difficulty learning new vocabulary can be put in groups of four to six children for additional small-group vocabulary lessons. The words that they need to learn can be entered on a *Vocabulary checklist* (Appendix 2) and ticked off as each child learns them.

❖ Teaching each word should normally continue until all children in the group have learned it (in the early years this may take several weeks). It does not matter if children are learning at different rates; these children will benefit from the extra practice. But if one or two children are having particular difficulty they should not delay the rest. They will need to be given whatever additional support the school or nursery can provide.

Getting started

Conversation skills

Listening skills

Narrative skills

Discussion skills

Reviewing progress and moving on (see Chapter 6)

❖ Staff can keep a running record of individual progress by entering children's names on the checklist and ticking off each skill or word as each child acquires it. A skill should not be credited until the child is using it *confidently*, *competently* and *consistently*.

❖ Staff should also review all children at the end of the term or the beginning of the next term, to bring records up to date and possibly reorganize teaching groups or move some children from one category to another. Teaching groups can also be reconsidered when starting a new checklist.

❖ Ideally, teaching of each checklist should continue until every child in the group or class has acquired all the skills on that checklist. This may not be possible by the end of term, in which case teaching of that checklist can continue into the next term.

At the end of the year

❖ Ideally, all children will at least have completed the second checklist by the end of the year. Children who are still very delayed at the end of the year may need special provision, such as further small-group work in the relevant skills, either in their current class or by returning to the previous year's class for some lessons.

❖ If a significant number of children have not completed the second checklist, or have barely begun the third, it may be sensible to continue teaching the current programme into the first term of the following year, and not introduce the next step until the second term.

❖ Staff should in any case liaise with staff for the following year and pass on the details of children who have not completed checklists, their likely progress, and any further support that they may need.

Getting started

Conversation skills

Listening skills

Narrative skills

Discussion skills

Conversation skills — Initial screen

Child's name	**Band 1**			**Band 2**			**Band 3**				Competent	Developing	Delayed
	Communicates with other children, verbally or non-verbally	Will talk to adults (may need encouragement)	Is combining two or more words most of the time	Greets familiar adults or children, for example by saying 'Hello'	Responds verbally to questions or comments	Talks spontaneously to adults or other children	Asks for help if needed	Can give an extended response of at least two sentences	Converses with adults or children in different situations				
TOTALS													

Children who have all the skills in Bands 1 and 2 and at least one skill from Band 3 are classified as *Competent*.

Children who have all the skills in Band 1 and at least one skill from Band 2 are classified as *Developing*.

All other children are classified as *Delayed* and should work on *Getting started* instead of *Conversation skills*.

Conversation skills

Early conversation skills

Child's name

Social contact

	Makes eye contact with familiar adults and children
	Greets familiar adults and children non-verbally, for example smiles
	Greets familiar adults and children verbally, for example says 'Hello'
	Says 'Goodbye' or similar to familiar adults and children

Listening and responding

	Looks at person speaking
	Listens and shows interest
	Responds non-verbally by nodding or shaking head
	Responds non-verbally with other action, for example following directions
	Responds verbally, by answering a question
	Responds verbally, by making an appropriate comment

Taking turns

	Takes turns in games and nursery routines
	Can play by passing on an object or message
	Waits for turn in games and circle activities
	Allows others to speak (waits for pauses, does not interrupt)

Checklist 1

Getting started

Conversation skills

Listening skills

Narrative skills

Discussion skills

One Step at a Time © Ann Locke (Network Continuum Education, 2006)

Conversation skills

Basic conversation skills

Child's name

Expressing needs and wants

| Can ask for help or permission when needed |
| Can ask or say when wants or needs something |
| Can ask or say when wants someone else to do something |

Initiating conversation

| Can initiate conversation non-verbally, for example by pointing or holding something up |
| Can initiate conversation verbally, by commenting on something |
| Can initiate conversation verbally, by asking a question |

Maintaining conversation

| Can continue a conversation, by commenting on what has been said |
| Can continue a conversation, by asking a question |
| Can give an extended response (at least two sentences) |
| Can maintain a conversation for at least three turns per person |
| Can keep to topic |

Conversation in everyday routines

| Regularly converses when dressing or undressing |
| Regularly converses when eating or drinking |
| Regularly converses when toileting or washing |
| Regularly converses while playing with other children |

Checklist 2

Getting started | Conversation skills | Listening skills | Narrative skills | Discussion skills

Conversation skills

Further conversation skills

Conversation skills

Child's name

Describing feelings, needs and wants

												Can talk about their current needs and wants
												Can talk about their feelings

Seeking clarification

												Indicates non-verbally if hasn't understood, for example by facial expression
												Indicates verbally if hasn't understood, for example by asking a question

Understanding reasons

												Can respond to reasons why or why not
												Can give reasons why or why not

Terminating a conversation

												Does not terminate conversations inappropriately, for example when someone else is still speaking
												Can terminate a conversation with an appropriate form of words, for example 'Thanks' or 'Goodbye'

Attempting repair

												Recognizes when others have not understood
												Attempts verbal repair, using the same or similar words
												Attempts verbal repair by trying to put the same thing differently

Checklist 3

Getting started

Conversation skills

Listening skills

Narrative skills

Discussion skills

Conversation skills

Vocabulary wordlist

Quality	Colour	Texture	Sound	Shape	Size	Quantity	Number	Space	Time	Movement	Feelings and emotion
dirty	black	cold	loud	circle	big	a bit	first	away	after	backwards	clever
easy	blue	dry	noisy	dot/spot	biggest	a lot	last	behind	again	fast	frightened
heavy	colour	hard	quiet	flat	little	as many	number	by	bedtime	go	funny
like	green	hot	sound	line	long	as much		down	birthday	move	good
new	red	soft		round	small	all		in	clock	quick	happy
warm	yellow	wet		straight	smallest	another one		in front	daytime	shake	hungry
				square		any		inside		slow	kind
						full		near		start	naughty
						many		next to		stop	nice
						more		on		still	pretty
						no more		on top			sad
						some		off			silly
								out			sorry
								outside			thirsty
								over			
								through			
								to			
								under			
								up			

Getting started | **Conversation skills** | Listening skills | Narrative skills | Discussion skills

Notes on Checklist 1:
Early conversation skills

This checklist features the early skills, some of them pre-verbal, that children need if they are to develop adequate conversation. Some of these skills are elementary and many children will have them already, but they may need to be taught and practised with some children.

Social contact

Knowing how to approach other people and make contact with them in an acceptable way is an important social skill, and a foundation of conversation with friends and with strangers. Some children may have to learn how to do this, using the behaviour of staff as a model.

These skills are most usefully taught in the context of daily nursery routines, especially at the beginning and end of the day, and through circle games, with children taking it in turns to practise smiling or saying 'Hello' or 'Goodbye'.

Listening and responding

Young children do not always recognize when an adult is talking to them: it literally goes over their heads. They may have to learn to attend, take in what is said, and to show that they are listening. Showing that you are listening by looking at the speaker or nodding your head is an important conversation skill. It can be very off-putting when someone you are talking to fails to respond in any way, and the conversation quickly breaks down.

Staff can use talk-time to explain to children why it is important to listen, and how they should respond to show they have heard and understood. They can then encourage and highlight the appropriate responses. Circle games can also be used to practise these skills, for example following directions, where each child in turn gives his neighbour an instruction such as 'Give a blue brick to Patti.' (from a box of coloured bricks in the middle of the circle) or answering questions, where each child in turn asks his neighbour a question such as 'What's your favourite food/drink/etc.?'

Taking turns

Turn-taking is an important social skill in all sorts of situations, not just in conversation. Children need to learn to wait their turn in any number of classroom and playground activities and they need to learn how to take turns in conversation, as speaker and as listener. Taking turns in play gives children an understanding of this procedure before they learn to use it in conversation. They also need to learn the cues through which we signal our readiness to switch roles from listener to speaker and back again. Some basic turn-taking skills are included in the *Getting started* programme and can also be used here.

Staff can use talk-time to discuss why turn-taking matters in general, for example in playing with toys or asking the teacher questions, and why it is important to listen and not interrupt in a conversation. Turn-taking in conversation can then be practised in talk-time and circle-time, as well as in daily nursery routines.

Notes on Checklist 2:
Basic conversation skills

This checklist includes the minimum skills that children need to engage in simple conversations.

Expressing needs and wants

Many children will indicate non-verbally when they need help or want something, for example by pointing, grunting or tugging at an adult. They need to learn how to use talk to make their needs and wants known, not only as a social skill – pointing and grunting is not normally considered acceptable – but because it is a more accurate and effective way of getting things done. This includes asking for help or permission, for example to go to the toilet, saying or asking when they want something ('Can I have the scissors/do some cutting?'), and saying or asking when they want others to do something for them ('Can you read me a story?').

Staff can use talk-time to discuss with children the ways they sometimes need help, and how they can ask for it. Where children are not expressing themselves verbally, staff can help either directly, by highlighting the skill in question ('Remember how we ask for something'), or indirectly, by giving their own verbal account of what the child is asking for ('What is it you want? Do you need help with your coat? Shall I help you to take it off?').

Initiating conversation

As well as responding to an adult's conversational moves, children also need to be able to initiate conversations themselves, with familiar adults and with other children. This needs a certain amount of self-confidence, so it is important that staff establish a warm and friendly relationship with each child.

When an adult has a child's confidence they will normally start to initiate conversation spontaneously, but some children may be slow to develop this skill. Frequent conversation initiated by an adult will help, and commenting on your own experience ('Wasn't it a lovely weekend? I sat in my back garden reading a book.') can be more effective in getting children to talk than asking them questions. But be prepared to be patient – it is important not to rush or push the child. It is virtually impossible to get children to talk if they don't want to!

Maintaining conversation

A conversation is more than just one or two exchanges between speakers. It requires a series of exchanges, with different people taking turns as speaker. Responses need to be appropriate and sensitively timed; a response that it is too quick or too slow can interfere with the flow of a conversation as surely as a failure to respond at all. Speakers also need to be able to keep to a topic without going off at a tangent, and changes of topic need to be signalled and smooth.

Staff can help children maintain a conversation by showing an interest in whatever the child is saying, and commenting on it or asking questions that are within the child's capacity to answer. In asking questions, open requests are better than closed questions, which have a determinate answer, for example 'That's a nice picture. Can you tell me about it?' rather than 'What's that you've painted?' At the end of any conversation staff should highlight and praise the child's contribution, for example 'That was interesting. I liked talking about your dog.' They should also comment on and praise any instances of children talking to each other, for example 'I saw you had a nice talk with Mary.'

Conversation in everyday routines

Children need to be able to use conversation in many different contexts, not just the situations where staff have been teaching conversation skills. Conversation occurs most easily in situations that are familiar and involving. At this age these will be the daily domestic and nursery routines, so these will be the situations where children have most to talk about and will find it easiest to talk.

Children should not be credited with these items unless they are conversing competently and confidently, frequently and freely, in the appropriate contexts. The crucial thing is the amount of conversation, not its accuracy or adequacy.

Notes on Checklist 3:
Further conversation skills

This checklist features more sophisticated conversation skills that normally take a long time to develop and will be present only in an elementary form at this age. They are quite subtle and may need to be introduced slowly and carefully. It does not matter if children do not master all the skills on this checklist. Terminating a conversation and attempting repair are likely to be particularly difficult and it may only be possible to introduce the general idea, explaining it and why it is important without expecting children to demonstrate the skill.

Describing feelings, needs and wants

Being able to recognize their own and other people's feelings is an essential social skill that children need if they are to cope with the complex demands of school life and other social interactions. Learning to describe their needs, wants and feelings as well as express them introduces them to the vocabulary of emotion and helps them understand what feelings, needs and wants are.

Staff can use talk-time to talk about the feelings that arise in different everyday situations and get children to talk about when they might feel happy or sad, or what makes them feel frightened or sorry. They can also use story-time to highlight and discuss the feelings of characters in a story. This is the best way to handle talk about negative emotions that children may find difficult or worrying.

Seeking clarification

Children need to understand how a conversation can break down, through misunderstanding or a failure to understand, and how it can be repaired. The first steps are being able to recognize that they haven't understood someone and having the confidence to seek clarification.

Staff can use talk-time to explain that we don't always understand what other people are saying. It is important to stress that this doesn't matter, it's not anyone's fault, and it is good to ask for more information: 'If you're not sure what I said, you can just put up your hand and ask.' Staff can also model uncertainty, verbally and non-verbally, even when they have understood, and praise any similar response from the child: 'That was sensible, asking me to explain it again.'

If a child fails to give the appropriate response, staff can encourage him with leading questions like 'Can you remember all that?' … 'Did you follow what I said?'… 'Would you like me to say it again?'

Understanding reasons

Being able to solve problems and negotiate behaviour through talk rather than conflict is an essential social – and classroom – skill. Learning how to reason and resolve conflicts through discussion takes many years. But as a first step, children need to recognize that others have feelings, needs and wants of their own, and recognize what their reasons are when they want others to do things or not to do them.

Staff can use story-time or talk-time to discuss how different people might have different wants, needs or feelings in the same situation, and how they might want different outcomes. Story-time can also be used to discuss the reasons why the characters might want to do something, or not want something to happen. Children's responses to questions about the characters' motivations will show if they have a grasp of their reasons for their actions. They can then be asked about the reasons for their own actions, why they want certain things to happen or not to happen, and whether these reasons will apply to everyone or be accepted by others.

Terminating conversation

This is another basic social skill. Children need to recognize when a conversation has finished, and to know how to end a conversation themselves in an acceptable way – and not, for example, just turning away or walking off, especially if somebody is still talking.

If a child does terminate a conversation inappropriately, this is an opportunity to explain why it was inappropriate and what the appropriate behaviour would be: 'Jason, I'm still talking. You should wait till I've finished.'

Staff can also model these skills by making it clear themselves when their own conversation has ended: 'I enjoyed that talk. Now it's time to …', 'Thank you. Now I need to talk to Mary.'

Attempting repair

Repair, or providing clarification, can be attempted either by repeating the same words or, more subtly, by trying to say the same thing in different words. At a more sophisticated level, speakers need to be able to recognize from non-verbal clues alone – a frown, a puzzled look, or simply a lack of attention – that the listener may not have understood. More subtly still, they need to recognize for themselves that the language they are using is difficult or inappropriate. (This last is a skill that staff also need to develop when teaching young children!)

Here too, staff can use talk-time to explain that we don't always make ourselves clear, and that we sometimes need to explain ourselves if others haven't understood us. They should also find or create opportunities to model repair: 'I didn't explain that very well. Let me try again.' They should also ask children for clarification whenever appropriate, using language that will help the child to respond appropriately: 'I'm not sure what you said you did. Can you tell me again?'

Getting started

Conversation skills

Listening skills

Narrative skills

Discussion skills

Eight tips for promoting talk with young children

1 **Create a context**

Adults and children do not talk about nothing. They discuss things of mutual concern arising from a shared activity. Conversation is almost always a by-product of shared experience, not an exercise in itself. Children are much more likely to talk about the things that are relevant to them and their lives. Trying to teach words out of context does not usually work. It is also easier to understand a child's utterances, and for the child to understand the adult, when talk surrounds a known context.

2 **Comment on activity**

Practical 'hands-on' experiences are the most likely to stimulate talk. Show an interest in what the child is doing and relate talk to the immediate context.

3 **Talk with, not at, the child**

Children should be genuine language partners even at a single-word level. Listen with genuine interest to what the child has to say and respond to what he has said, then hand the conversation back, helping him to explore the topic further, and give him time to reply. Conversation can often be sustained if the adult gives 'phatic responses' or 'social oil' like 'Hmm, that looks interesting.' or 'Ooh, that looks good.'

4 **Reflect and expand**

If the child gives a word or short sentence, respond by restating, extending and slightly expanding it, for example the child says 'hot' and the adult replies 'Yes, it is hot. That's the kettle.' The adult maintains the conversation by checking the child's meaning and making it explicit, expanding the child's contribution and adding relevant vocabulary, and generally discussing and negotiating meaning despite the limited language under the child's control.

5 **Don't overload**

Keep the conversation at the child's level, using words or constructions that he should be able to understand.

6 **Be personal**

Give personal contributions related to the child's experience and what the child knows, for example 'Yesterday I had a surprise too.' or 'See, I've fastened your lace.'

7 **Avoid correcting**

Avoid interrupting, correcting or asking the child to repeat or rephrase a sentence. Asking a child to correct a phrase ('say *I did*, not *I done*') or faulty pronunciation ('*crisp* not *cwisp*') is usually very inhibiting. Restate what the child is trying to say, but go for meaning rather than correct language.

8 **Don't cross-examine**

Take care with questions. Yes/no questions like 'Do you want to play with it?' do little to stimulate children's language. Test questions like 'What colour are your socks?' or open questions like 'What did you do at the weekend?' may fail to get any response at all. Questions offering alternatives like 'Are they blue or red?' or 'Do you want me to fasten it or leave it undone?' are easier and more helpful.

(Adapted from Webster, A. (1987), 'Enabling language acquisition: The developmental evidence', *Division of Educational and Child Psychology Newsletter*, 27, pp.27–31, Leicester, British Psychological Society

Getting started

Conversation skills

Listening skills

Narrative skills

Discussion skills

11

Listening skills

Listening is a complex skill. It includes hearing, attending, understanding and remembering. Children begin to develop these skills from an early age, not just in conversation but also from listening to songs, rhymes and stories and listening to talk about pictures and stories as well as about the things around them. The ability to follow a story becomes essential when children learn to read, and eventually to write.

Children who have not had these experiences may lack these skills. Some may have poor hearing that has not been identified. Others may have difficulty attending, understanding or remembering. Others, especially if they come from the *Conversation skills* step in the programme, may have to learn to stop talking and start listening!

The most fundamental skill that children need at school is the ability to understand basic classroom language. They need to understand simple questions and be able to follow simple directions and instructions if they are to learn anything at all in the classroom. Teachers need to ensure that all children have these skills.

However, children also need to learn a different type of listening from the listening they are used to at home. Most listening at home is listening to conversations that are between a few people who know each other well and are about current experiences and familiar routines. It is direct, face-to-face and involves eye contact with one or two people. Children are expected to respond and be able to interrupt, which enables adults to monitor children's understanding and to adjust their own language to an appropriate level. This conversational listening continues at nursery and school in small-group and one-to-one teaching, but most listening at school is very different.

At school, adults talk to a group or a whole class, not just individual children. Children may have to listen in a bigger space, with more children around them, than they are used to. They may be at a distance from the person who is speaking, and sitting while the speaker is standing. They may be listening to unfamiliar adults talking about unfamiliar things. Without the face-to-face eye contact they are used to, they may even think that all this talk has nothing to do with them. They also have to learn to listen for longer periods (extended listening) without responding until they're told to ('Quiet now! Sit still and listen.') They may have to remember what was said some considerable time before ('Does everyone remember what we talked about yesterday?') It may be about things that happened hours, days or weeks ago, or things that haven't happened yet. Even the content may be different from what they are used to. The purpose of much school talk is precisely to introduce new information, new material or new activities. This is a different, more intensive and more focused type of listening that all children need to acquire but which some find difficult.

Listening skills are crucial for literacy. Schools are currently under considerable pressure to introduce children to reading as soon as possible. Yet many children starting school are simply not ready because they lack the necessary auditory skills. They need to be able to discriminate word sounds and syllables in order to establish the link between letters and sounds; they need to be able to understand what is said to them in order to understand what they read; and they need to be able to follow a story in order to produce a coherent text themselves. Helping children to listen, understand and follow should be essential steps in a school's literacy strategy.

Children need to be able to hear the difference between different syllables and word sounds if they are to grasp phonics and use them in reading, writing and spelling. They typically acquire these skills from musical games and activities, playing with sound-making toys and instruments, listening to and learning nursery rhymes and songs, and playing word-sound games like 'I spy'. Children who lack these skills may learn to read by recognizing words as wholes, but will later have problems with spelling because they cannot break the words down into separate sounds.

Children also need to understand what they hear. Some children learn the mechanics of reading in the sense that they can turn the written symbols into sounds, but they still have little idea of what they are reading. This often does not become obvious until the later primary years when they have to use their reading to learn and find things out for themselves. Children who have difficulty following spoken language will also have difficulty understanding what they are reading. The better their understanding of spoken language, the better their reading comprehension will be and the more they will learn from what they read. 'The inspection evidence … shows the importance of an emphasis on spoken language and the experience of being read to in many of the most effective schools. These help pupils to develop a vocabulary and an understanding of narrative or the structure of other texts, which they need to supplement phonic knowledge in order to read with full comprehension' (Ofsted, 2005).

Extended listening without the support of a conversational partner also prepares children for writing. But to follow a story or other text we have to do more than understand the words and sentences; we also have to understand how they fit together and make a whole. Children who have not had regular bedtime stories or stories read to them at other times, may have difficulty with the very idea of a story where a series of events follow one another. Television is no substitute because the programmes (and the adverts!) are often episodic, relying on exciting incidents to hold children's attention rather than a story line, if indeed there is one. If children seem bored, distracted or naughty during story-time – or even if they are sitting quietly and passively – they may simply not be understanding what the teacher is talking about.

Moreover, understanding a story or other account usually involves more than understanding what is actually written or said (explicit or surface meaning); we also have to be able to read or listen 'between the lines' (implicit or contextual meaning). We usually have to add a great deal of background knowledge and personal experience about the world and the way it works, about people and the way they work. Storytelling and any form of extended writing would be impossible if we had to be precise and explicit about everything – in the way we sometimes do have to explain everything to very young children.

One particularly important form of this understanding is recognizing why the characters in a story behave as they do, what they are feeling and why they are feeling it, all of which is often implicit. It usually gets taken for granted that children will understand why a character is angry or sad, is crying or running away. But teachers who ask their class – or better, a small group – 'Why was the boy crying?' or 'Why did she get angry?' may be surprised at the answers. This type of understanding is obviously important for children's social and emotional development and their understanding of their own and other people's feelings and behaviour. But it is also needed for other subjects such as early science, for example to understand why some animals hide or run away, come out at night or live in trees.

Children who have completed the *Listening skills* step in the programme should be ready for the more formal types of learning they will meet in later years. They will be familiar with group listening and able to follow directions and instructions, to answer questions and follow lengthy accounts and explanations. They will have the foundations for literacy, especially reading; they will enjoy listening to and learning stories, songs and rhymes; they will recognize how sounds are used to form and spell out words; and they will be able to follow, interpret and learn from stories and factual accounts.

Initial screening (see Chapter 6)

Procedure

❖ Once children have settled into their new class, staff should spend at least a week observing their spoken language in a variety of situations, both formal and informal, and focusing on the skills that are to be assessed.

❖ Staff should then complete the initial screen for all the children in their class or group. This should be done in discussion with colleagues, in pairs or threes or in a staff meeting.

❖ Each screen is divided into three bands, and children are assessed band by band. This means that if children do not have all the skills in Band 1, they do not need to be assessed on Band 2; and if they do not have all the skills in Band 2, they do not need to be assessed on Band 3.

❖ A skill should be credited only if a child is using it *confidently*, *competently* and *consistently*. If there is any doubt or disagreement, or if the child's use of the particular skill is irregular or infrequent, it should not be credited. At this stage it is better to underestimate children's abilities than overestimate them.

❖ Children who have all the skills in Bands 1 and 2 and at least one skill in Band 3 are identified as reasonably *Competent* in the relevant skills.

Getting started

Conversation skills

Listening skills

Narrative skills

Discussion skills

Procedure

❖ Children who have all the skills in Band 1 and at least one skill in Band 2 are identified as *Developing* the relevant skills.

❖ All other children, that is, children who do not have all the skills in Band 1 and at least one skill in Band 2, are identified as *Delayed* in the relevant skills.

Note that children who do not have all the skills in Band 1 count as *Delayed* even if they have more than one skill in Band 2; and that children who do not have all the skills in Band 2 still count as *Developing* even if they have more than one skill in Band 3.

Using the skills checklists (see Chapter 6)

There are three checklists. *Understanding questions and instructions* deals with children's understanding of basic classroom language. *Hearing sound and word patterns* introduces the auditory skills that children need if they are to benefit from the phonics approach to reading and spelling. *Understanding meaning* deals with children's understanding of stories and other texts.

Procedure

❖ Staff should work through each checklist in turn, focusing on just a few items at a time. Each skill should be made an explicit teaching objective for one or more weeks, to ensure that all staff focus on that skill with all children and in all relevant activities, across the day and through the week.

❖ This can be a rolling programme of three or four skills at a time. This means that the class starts with one or two skills in the first week, adds another one or two in the second week, then replaces one or two with new skills in the third week, and so on.

❖ The sequence of skills in the checklist is meant only as a guide. Intervention should also be guided by the skills that children are developing spontaneously. In teaching one skill staff will often have been introducing another, and this can provide an easy transition from one skill to the next.

❖ Staff may find it helpful to identify in advance the skills they are going to teach and the order in which they are going to teach them, and build them into their advance planning, so lessons can be prepared, resources gathered and support staff guided in their work with small groups or individual children. But planning needs to be flexible because some skills may take longer to learn than expected, and some weeks should be left free so that staff can go back and repeat or reinforce any skills that children have been finding difficult.

❖ A list of the skills selected for current teaching should be displayed prominently in the classroom so all staff can refer to them and encourage and reinforce them at all times during the day.

Classroom intervention (see Chapter 6)

Small-group work in a quiet area where children will not be distracted or disturbed is particularly important for developing listening skills, especially the phonic skills in *Checklist 2: Hearing sound and word patterns*. The size of the group is also important, with children who are having particular difficulty needing to be taught in a smaller group.

Listening work should also be included in other classroom teaching, several times a day. It does not need a separate or special lesson. Regular classroom activities like story-time, circle-time, music and PE lessons can all be used to develop and extend children's listening skills; clearing up or getting ready to go outdoors can be used to reinforce children's ability to follow a sequence of instructions; a few spare minutes before break can be used to practise nursery rhymes.

Procedure

❖ Each skill should be introduced, explained and/or demonstrated to the class or group as a whole before being made the focus of small-group work. When introducing any new skill or activity it is always good practice to explain what it is that children need to learn, and why they need to learn it. If children know what is expected of them they are much more likely to exhibit the behaviour in question.

❖ There should then be at least one whole-class activity every day focusing on the skills currently being learned. These need not be separate or special lessons – they can be curriculum lessons, circle-time or story-time, activities like art and design, PE or music – but the class teacher should identify at least one specific occasion each day when staff will model, encourage and reinforce the relevant skills for all children, not just those receiving small-group work.

❖ All staff should be encouraged to use every other opportunity through the day, including playtime and dinnertime, to model, encourage and reinforce these skills with individual children.

Small-group work

❖ Each group should be of four to six children. As far as possible, the same member of staff should always lead each group.

❖ Children identified as *Delayed* should be given 10–15 minutes small-group listening work every day if possible, certainly two or three times a week. Children identified as *Developing* should be given 10–15 minutes small-group language work at least once a week. Children identified as *Competent* should also be given small-group work whenever possible.

❖ It is usually convenient to group the children identified as *Delayed*, and the children identified as *Developing*, because that is easier to schedule and makes it easier to support and monitor the children most in need of it. But children will also benefit from mixed-ability groupings. Absences can give opportunities to include *Competent* or *Developing* children in the *Developing* or *Delayed* groups.

❖ The same groupings can be used as for other purposes but language teaching should be additional to other small-group work. Groups can be reorganized if children progress at different rates through the year.

Getting started
Conversation skills
Listening skills
Narrative skills
Discussion skills

Procedure

❖ Small-group teaching should proceed at a pace that includes every child. It is better to consolidate a skill for all children than to push ahead too quickly. It does not matter if children are learning at different rates – all children will benefit from the extra practice. However if some children are still learning a skill after three or more weeks, it may be sensible to leave it for a while and come back to it again later.

❖ Teaching a particular skill should normally continue until all the children in that group have learned it, but if one or two children are having particular difficulty they should not delay the rest. They will need whatever additional support the school can provide. If several children in the class are having difficulty it may be necessary to continue teaching that skill to these children, and possibly the whole class, for longer than originally planned.

Teaching method

Teaching listening skills is not difficult but it does need time and attention. The more limited children's experience at home – if, for example, they are not familiar with nursery rhymes, or have not had regular bedtime stories – the more support they will need at school. Repetition is particularly important (see Chapter 3). Staff sometimes think they need to keep changing the stories they read to a class to retain children's interest and broaden their experience. But at this age the same story can be told every day for at least a week without children becoming bored. Indeed, it may not be until the third, fourth, or even fifth, telling that some children begin to take in what the story is about. Similarly, nursery rhymes and songs may need to be repeated for days, even weeks, before some children will know all the words.

Another key factor is the choice of material. It pays to build up a repertoire of material and activities, graded by difficulty, before teaching begins. This material needs to be interesting to the children, and at a level they can understand. Rhymes and songs can use unfamiliar or nonsense language because the rhythm and pace will carry children along, but stories and word or sound games need to use language that relates closely to the children's own lives and experience. Pictures, toys, objects and other visual prompts can help children understand verbal information. Teachers also need to be sensitive to children's current level of language and to adjust their own language accordingly, always relating it to activities that are familiar to the children they are working with.

Finally, although these children will have to learn how to listen in surroundings that are often less than optimal, initial teaching needs to be in situations that are quiet and comfortable, especially when children are acquiring new skills or if they are experiencing difficulty. Staff should also keep an eye out for undiagnosed hearing problems. Ear infections, such as 'glue ear', are very common at this age and can have a serious effect on children's learning and social interaction.

The following are the key teaching techniques (see Chapter 6).

◆ *Modelling*: the adult demonstrates the skill she wants children to learn, for example clapping in time to music or clapping out the rhythm of words or phrases. Imitation is a powerful means of teaching and learning.

◆ *Highlighting*: the adult draws attention to the relevant skill by discussing it, emphasizing its importance, or explaining how, when or why we use it, for example when and why we need to listen carefully, or why it is difficult to follow a complex instruction. She can also do this by asking questions – 'How do we find rhyming words?' – discussing the children's responses, and then summarizing and highlighting the key points: 'We listen to all the words and try to find ones that sound the same at the end.'

◆ *Prompting*: the adult encourages the child to respond, directing him towards the appropriate behaviour: 'Can you tell what is happening in this picture?' … 'Did that ever happen to you?'

◆ *Rewarding*: the adult rewards appropriate responses with praise and further encouragement. If the praise can emphasize what was good about the response – 'That's good. You *were* listening well.' … 'Well done, you remembered everything that happened.' – it will help children recognize what it is you want them to learn. If a response is not quite what the adult is looking for, she can encourage a more appropriate response by asking questions, prompting or modelling the skill again.

Vocabulary teaching (see Chapter 7)

The *Listening skills* vocabulary consists mostly of adjectives, prepositions and some basic curriculum nouns that children need to know in Reception, selected from early cross-curricular vocabulary and the vocabulary of feelings and emotion. Many children will know most of these words already but they should not be taken for granted, especially with children whose spoken language is less developed.

Children will find these words more difficult to grasp than the concrete nouns and verbs of their early vocabulary but they will learn them, too, through practical involvement with real objects. This is particularly important with prepositions: children learn words like *backwards* or *beside* by moving things – or, even better, moving themselves – backwards or beside something. Quantity terms can also be taught through practical activities, for example putting *a few* bricks in the box or putting water in a glass until it is *nearly* full. Adjectives should also be introduced and explained using concrete examples that children can handle for themselves (an *old* book, a *rough* blanket). Nouns can be taught by doing something or by making things (using a *penny* to buy something or drawing a *triangle*).

Getting started

Conversation skills

Listening skills

Narrative skills

Discussion skills

Procedure

❖ Staff should identify 6–10 words for teaching each week as 'this week's special words'. As well as words chosen from current curriculum topics, they should include between two and four words from the *Listening skills* vocabulary list. If children are finding some words difficult they can be featured over several weeks, or repeated at different times during the year.

❖ It will usually be convenient to teach a selection of words from the same category (quality, colour, etc.) at the same time, but staff should avoid words that are similar in sound or meaning (for example *late* and *later*, *each* and *every*) and contrasting pairs (for example *deep* and *shallow*, *high* and *low*), which some children will find confusing.

❖ The words for the week should be introduced and explained to the whole class at the beginning of the week, and displayed prominently in the classroom for reference by children as well as by staff.

❖ These words should then be included and featured by all staff on every possible occasion over the rest of the week, in whole-class lessons, group work, one-to-one interaction and classroom routines. Children who have begun to read can support their own learning by being encouraged to consult the list of this week's words, look out for them in their lessons and reading, and use them in their own talk and writing.

❖ Towards the end of the week staff should monitor the learning of all children and identify any words that seem to be proving particularly difficult. Children who are slow in acquiring new vocabulary should be checked individually.

❖ The crucial test is that these children understand the word in question, whether or not they are using it (they may be copying other children). Understanding can be checked by asking questions, or by giving instructions and seeing if children respond appropriately, while making sure that they are not following other children.

❖ Any children who have difficulty learning new vocabulary can be put in groups of four to six children for additional small-group vocabulary lessons. The words they need to learn can be entered on a *Vocabulary checklist* (Appendix 2) and ticked off as each child learns them.

❖ Teaching each word should normally continue until all children in the group have learned it (in the early years this may take several weeks). It does not matter if children are learning at different rates; these children will benefit from the extra practice. But if one or two children are having particular difficulty they should not delay the rest. They will need to be given whatever additional support that the school or nursery can provide.

Getting started   Conversation skills   Listening skills   Narrative skills   Discussion skills

Reviewing progress and moving on (see Chapter 6)

Procedure

❖ Staff can keep a running record of individual progress by entering children's names on the checklist and ticking off each skill or word as each child acquires it. A skill should not be credited until the child is using it *confidently*, *competently* and *consistently*.

❖ Staff should also review all children at the end of the term or the beginning of the next term, to bring records up to date and possibly reorganize teaching groups or move some children from one category to another. Teaching groups can also be reconsidered when starting a new checklist.

❖ Ideally, teaching of each checklist should continue until every child in the group or class has acquired all the skills on that checklist. This may not be possible by the end of term, in which case teaching of that checklist can continue into the next term.

At the end of the year

❖ Ideally, all children will at least have completed the second checklist by the end of the year. Children who are still very delayed at the end of the year may need special provision, such as further small-group work in the relevant skills, either in their current class or by returning to the previous year's class for some lessons.

❖ If a significant number of children have not completed the second checklist, or have barely begun the third, it may be sensible to continue teaching the current programme into the first term of the following year, and not introduce the next step until the second term.

❖ Staff should in any case liaise with staff for the following year and pass on the details of children who have not completed checklists, their likely progress, and any further support that they may need.

Listening skills

Initial screen

Child's name	Band 1			Band 2			Band 3				Competent	Developing	Delayed
	Can follow simple instructions	Will join in simple nursery rhymes	Can follow a simple story	Can follow familiar instructions that are given to the whole class	Can answer simple questions	Can follow a longer story told to the whole class	Learns new nursery rhymes easily	Can follow unfamiliar instructions given to the whole class	Can follow an unfamiliar story told to the whole class		Competent	Developing	Delayed
										TOTALS			

Children who have all the skills in Bands 1 and 2 and at least one skill from Band 3 are classified as *Competent*.

Children who have all the skills in Band 1 and at least one skill from Band 2 are classified as *Developing*.

All other children are classified as *Delayed*.

Side tabs: Getting started · Conversation skills · **Listening skills** · Narrative skills · Discussion skills

Understanding questions and instructions

Child's name

Early question forms

Understands *What's that?*											
Understands *What is/are … doing?*											
Understands *Where is …?*											
Understands *Who is …?*											
Understands *Who can …?*											

Following instructions

Can follow a simple instruction											
Can follow an instruction to fetch two objects											
Can follow an instruction to fetch three objects											
Can follow a sequence of familiar instructions											
Can follow a sequence of less familiar instructions											

Later question forms

Understands *What's that for?*											
Understands *When?*											
Understands *Why?*											
Understands *How?*											

Checklist 1

Getting started | Conversation skills | **Listening skills** | Narrative skills | Discussion skills

Getting started
Conversation skills
Listening skills
Narrative skills
Discussion skills

Listening skills

Hearing sound and word patterns

Child's name

Hearing rhythms and rhymes

Skill											
Can join in action-word games and rhymes											
Can do the correct actions in action games											
Can march in time to music											
Can clap in time to music or songs											
Knows at least 10 nursery rhymes by heart											
Can complete the rhyme, in familiar rhymes											

Identifying sounds

Can recognize at least 10 animals or objects by the sounds that they make											
Can identify an object or musical instrument by its sound, out of two											
Can identify an object or musical instrument by its sound, out of three											
Can repeat a sequence of two sounds, using instruments or objects											
Can repeat a sequence of three sounds, using instruments or objects											

Discriminating sounds in words

Skill											
Can clap out the rhythm of a word or phrase											
Given a word, can repeat the initial sound											
Given a sound, can find a word that begins with it											
Can play 'I spy'											
Can find new rhyming words											
Given a word, can repeat the final sound											

Using word memory

Skill											
Can play memory games, remembering three items											
Can play memory games, remembering four items											

Checklist 2

Listening skills

Understanding meaning

Listening skills

Child's name

Understanding pictures

Can name people and objects in picture scenes										
Can describe what is happening in picture scenes										

Understanding stories

Can name characters or objects in a picture story										
Can name characters or objects in a story without using the pictures										
Can say what is happening in a picture story										
Can say what is happening in a story without using the pictures										
Can say what happens next in a familiar story using the pictures										
Can say what happens next in a familiar story without using the pictures										

Understanding time

Can comment on or answer questions about current events										
Can comment on or answer questions about past events										
Understands 'What will happen next?'										
Understands 'What will happen if …?'										

Understanding implicit meanings

Can identify objects, animals, etc. from a verbal description										
Can link picture scenes to personal experience										
Can link events in a story to personal experience										
Can offer an explanation of what is going on in a picture scene										
Can offer an explanation of what is going on in a story										

Checklist 3

Getting started

Conversation skills

Listening skills

Narrative skills

Discussion skills

Listening skills

Vocabulary wordlist

Quality	Colour	Texture	Sound	Shape	Size	Quantity	Number	Space	Time	Movement	Feelings and emotion
dark	brown	rough	high	cross	bigger	a few	both	above	always	along	afraid
different	orange	smooth	loudly	pattern	deep	each	fifth	across	before	around	angry
light	pink		low	shape	fat	enough	fourth	against	early	forwards	bad
old	white		quietly	star	large	every	half	below	late	sideways	beautiful
plain			silent	triangle	longest	less	next	beside	later	towards	cross
same			soft		shallow	most	penny	between	never	cross	excited
striped					short	much	pound	bottom	sometimes		friendly
					thin	none	second	close (to)	summer		helpful
					nearly	plenty	third	facing	winter		lovely
						several	twice	far			nasty
						very		high			pleased
						whole		low			surprised
								middle			tired
								(a) space			uncomfortable
								together			unkind
								top			

Getting started | Conversation skills | **Listening skills** | Narrative skills | Discussion skills

Notes on Checklist 1:
Understanding questions and instructions

This checklist deals with children's understanding of simple classroom language. Most Reception children will have these skills already, but teachers need to ensure that all children have them. Note that at this point the emphasis is on children's understanding of language rather than its use. Children's use of question forms – asking questions for themselves – is dealt with at the next step of the programme, *Narrative skills*.

Understanding can be difficult to monitor, especially in whole-class activities. If children do not respond it is easy to assume that they have not been paying attention; their failure to understand gets misdiagnosed as a failure to attend. If they have poor auditory memories or find it difficult to keep up with rapid spoken language they may develop coping strategies, for example using visual clues or knowledge of classroom routines. They may not be following what is said, merely following other children. Even the fact that they are using a word or expression does not necessarily mean that they understand it. Some children learn to say the appropriate thing by copying adults or other children without properly understanding what they are saying. Understanding is best monitored in the to-and-fro of one-to-one conversation, where adults can tell from children's responses how much they really understand.

Early question forms

The best way to teach questions is to select one at a time and display it in a prominent position as 'this week's question'. The teacher should then explain this question in a whole-class or large-group lesson, getting the children to talk about when they might use it and what it helps them to find out. It can then be featured in classroom teaching wherever possible, especially circle-time or when talking about stories or pictures, with the teacher modelling, encouraging and reinforcing children's use of the question, as described above. Although the question will be changed each week, the class can come back to the same one several times. It does not matter if most children already know it. Teachers can introduce more complex questions with those children, while targeting the current question at those who are still learning it.

Another useful aid is a 'questions table' with a variety of interesting and intriguing objects or with pictures that staff and children can use as a basis for asking the question of the week. As well as whole-class or group work, where the teacher uses the table to model and elicit this week's question, there can be times when children work at the table in pairs or small groups, with or without adult support, and ask each other questions about the objects on display. The display will alter as the question changes. Children can be encouraged to bring their own items to school to add to the table.

Following instructions

The ability to follow instructions is not just an essential classroom skill in its own right; it also helps to develop children's memories, including their auditory memories.

Teaching can begin with simple instructions like 'Bring me that book.' It can then move to complex instructions for familiar routines like 'Put on your coat and gloves, and go and

Getting started

Conversation skills

Listening skills

Narrative skills

Discussion skills

stand by the door.' Finally it can progress to unfamiliar complex instructions like 'Go and get a red ball and a blue ball from the basket and give one to your partner.' Break-time, playground games, PE and music sessions provide excellent opportunities for teaching instructions and directions.

Children who have difficulty following directions may have poor auditory attention or poor memory for speech. They can be helped by putting together a collection of pictures, objects or shapes, and giving simple instructions like 'find something blue', building up to a more complex instructions like 'Point to something in the picture, then find something like it on the table.' These activities can be fun for children, are easily managed in small-group sessions, and will help them to remember sequences of actions. It is important, however, to proceed slowly, and not to move to complex instructions too quickly. It can help if the teacher draws up a list of instructions in order of difficulty, and works through them one at a time, introducing the next instruction only when children are ready.

For more detailed suggestions for small-group activities see the Activities Handbook in *Teaching Talking* (Locke and Beech, 2005), Chapter 2.

Later question forms

These can be more difficult to introduce, but familiar household or kitchen items like a ball of string, a shopping bag, rubber bands or sticky tape can be used to ask 'What's this for?' or 'Why/how do we use this?' Pictures showing familiar family scenes can be used to ask 'When do we eat toast/clean our teeth?' and so on.

Notes on Checklist 2:
Hearing sound and word patterns

This checklist develops children's discrimination of sound and word patterns in preparation for the teaching of phonics in school reading programmes. It is not itself a phonics programme but a way of ensuring that all children have the abilities they need for using phonics. The importance of phonics in teaching reading is widely recognized but the underlying abilities are not so well understood. However, this checklist can be used in conjunction with, or as part of, a phonics-teaching programme. Many of the activities and some of the skills will be the same.

Some of the activities will in any case be familiar in every Reception classroom and should be part of normal teaching throughout the year. In particular, learning songs and nursery rhymes should be included in whole-class teaching from early in the first term. When children are working through this part of the programme these activities should be featured in whole-class teaching and small-group work every day, to ensure that all children in the class acquire the relevant skills and to give some children the extra practice that they need.

For more detailed suggestions for small-group activities see the Activities Handbook in *Teaching Talking* (Locke and Beech, 2005), Chapters 2 and 9.

Hearing rhythms and rhymes

Simple speech-action games like 'Miss Polly had a dolly' or 'This is the church and this is the steeple' encourage children to listen to the sound of words. Clapping, moving or marching in time to music helps them to hear the rhythm of words and syllables. Most Reception children should have these skills but, if not, they will need to be taught explicitly.

Nursery rhymes encourage children to enjoy the sound of words and recognize different word sounds, and help to develop their auditory memory. They can be taught in a rolling programme, with new rhymes introduced one by one, and no more than three being learned at any one time. Each rhyme should be repeated every day for at least three weeks. By the second term most children will already know several rhymes or songs, and it should not be necessary to check that they all know at least 10. For children classified as *Developing* or *Competent* it should be enough to check that they can learn new rhymes easily.

Children who are having difficulty learning nursery rhymes will need to be taught them in small-group sessions. The rhymes currently being taught in small-group work should also be featured daily in whole-class teaching.

Getting children to complete familiar rhymes - 'Hey diddle diddle, the cat and the …?' or 'Little Jack Horner sat in the …?' – is a way of tuning them into word sound patterns and will introduce them to the idea of words that rhyme or 'sound the same'.

Identifying sounds

Before children can learn to recognize and identify the sounds in words they need to be able to recognize natural sounds, and to identify things around them by the sound they make. This helps to develop auditory discrimination and auditory memory.

Most children will be able to identify simple 'nursery' sounds like *bow-wow*, *tick-tock* or *brrmm-brrmm*, though some children may need to be taught them. But they should also be introduced to natural sounds – clocks, cars, birds, etc. – in the classroom and outside ('What do you think is making that noise?') If the teacher makes a tape-recording of familiar sounds, she can play it back and see if children can identify the sounds without having the thing itself as a clue.

Musical instruments, or collections of tins or boxes containing beans, buttons, wooden blocks or nails, so they each make a different noise, can be used to teach children to identify sequences of sounds and then repeat them. At first they can watch as the teacher makes the sounds but eventually they should be able to identify the sounds without seeing what the teacher is doing. More able children can be taught to copy different rhythmic patterns as well.

Discriminating sounds in words

Auditory discrimination – the ability to separate the sounds that go to make up words – is essential for phonics work, and eventually for reading, writing and spelling.

Children can be helped to separate syllables and word and letter sounds by clapping out the rhythms of familiar words and phrases, for example *cro-co-dile*, *salt-and-pe-pper*.

Most children of this age should be able to identify and repeat the initial sound in a word, though the target sound may need to be emphasized at first: *mmm-mouse*, *sss-sand*. Finding a word that begins with a given sound is more difficult, because they have to think of a word while remembering the sound. Playing 'I spy', using pictures or objects in the room or outside, is a useful way of reinforcing and developing these skills. At first the teacher leads, with the children having to find a word that begins with that sound. Then the children can take it in turns to lead. They will find this more difficult, because they have to find an object, remember its name, and isolate the initial sound – all without giving it away!

Most children will also find it difficult to identify the final sounds in words: *run-n*, *hill-l*. A useful first step is being able to recognize simple single-syllable rhymes. At first the teacher may have to give several rhyming words before helping them find another: *hat–mat*, *pat–cat*, *red–head*, *said–bed*. But as children grow more familiar with the activity, they should be able to find rhymes for a single word: *far–car*, *now–cow*. Rhyming puzzles and rhyming cards (with pictures of things with rhyming names) can be helpful here.

Finding a word that ends with a given sound is too difficult for many children at this stage.

Using word memory

Memory games help to develop children's memory in general – essential for all learning – as well as their memories for words and meanings.

Games like 'I went shopping and I bought a ...' or 'I went on the bus and I saw a ...' can be introduced in circle-time or in small-group sessions. If some children find these games difficult try simpler games like 'Copy me' or 'What did I forget?' In 'Copy me' the teacher gets each child to repeat a simple phrase like *very silly boys*, *soon be bedtime* or *two tiny toes*. The teacher then asks the children to copy a sentence like *We are going to the shop to buy some bread* or *We had bread and jam for our tea*; then a list like *hands, feet, toes* or *bus, car, truck*. In 'What did I forget?' the teacher puts several objects on a table, names them all except one, and the child has to say which one got left out.

Notes on Checklist 3:
Understanding meaning

This checklist deals with children's understanding of narrative, time and implicit meaning. It will also help them develop the extended listening that they need in school and is very different from the conversational listening they will be used to at home.

Normally the teacher can select a mixture of skills from different parts of a checklist but in this case it is best to work through the skills in sequence, except as noted. Many of the skills overlap, so one skill will lead naturally to another. The choice of material is more than usually important, and teachers will find it useful to put aside a set of storybooks or other texts to be used specifically for teaching understanding, together with a list of questions that can be used to explore, first the literal meaning, then the implicit meanings. These questions should be graded by difficulty, and introduced one by one over the course of the term. It will also help to have a table with a set of pictures, toys or other objects illustrating or relevant to the current story, as well as the book itself, to encourage children to talk about the story, and to 'read' it themselves or to other children.

Understanding pictures

Pictures are easier to understand than texts, so they are the place to start. They should be 'picture scenes', that is, pictures with something going on, and more than one person or item, not just a single object. Children should first be asked to identify people or things in the picture ('What's that?' or 'Who do you think that lady is?'), then to describe what is happening or going on ('What is the boy doing?') As they progress the pictures can become more complex and detailed. Children need to be able to handle moderately complex pictures before moving to understanding stories.

Understanding stories

Telling children stories is a key way in which we teach them about people (or animals) and how they behave. It is also a valuable way of showing them the pleasures of reading. First, however, they need to be able to follow the story.

The teacher can start by using the pictures to ask questions about the characters while she is telling the story. She reads a bit, then checks understanding by asking questions, for example 'Who's this?' … 'What has he got?' Then she can ask these questions without using the pictures as a clue: 'Who knocked at the door?' … 'Who climbed up the beanstalk?' Questions that come at the end of a story will be more difficult for children to answer because they have to remember what happened. Teachers can try this – beginning with the same questions that they asked earlier – but should not expect all children to respond, especially at first. The next step is to see whether children can say what is happening in the story, first using the pictures, then without them. Finally, the teacher should check their understanding of the sequence of events by telling part of the story and asking 'What happens now?' or 'What happened next?'

Children who have difficulty holding a narrative in their head, or who seem not to have the idea of following a narrative, can be helped by using felt or magnetic boards to build up a story step by step, or sets of picture cards that can be laid out in sequence to tell a story. It

Getting started

Conversation skills

Listening skills

Narrative skills

Discussion skills

can also be very effective to use a camera to create your own sequences of pictures of familiar domestic activities or classroom routines, especially if the pictures can include the children themselves. At this stage children are not expected to put the pictures in sequence or tell the story themselves. As always, they should be praised if they do this spontaneously, but it is not the key objective here.

Understanding time

Children first use language in relation to present events and the things that they can currently see and hear. It takes time for them to develop and understand language that refers to the past, and especially the future. This goes hand in hand with the development of verb tenses.

Children's understanding of present, past and future can be monitored and developed through the sort of questioning that occurs in all classroom work. If closer monitoring is needed, it can be done by questioning children about stories or other texts. A good way of promoting an understanding of time is to have a large pictorial timetable on permanent display, showing all the days of the week including the weekend, and use it to talk about future, current and past events and activities. This will also model and promote the use of verb tenses and other time vocabulary, and encourage children to organize and plan their work and other activities.

Understanding *What will happen next?* or *What will happen if …?* is more complex than understanding tenses but is a crucial step towards science and more sophisticated writing. At first these questions should be about familiar activities in the classroom or outside, but they can later be extended to pictures and stories.

Understanding implicit meaning

Children need to understand the meanings behind pictures and stories, including why the characters behave as they do: 'Some children were going out to play. Their mother said, "Put your coats and boots on". Why do you think she said that?'

Children first need to be able to identify people, animals and objects from just a description, without using pictures. Then they should be able to explain what is going on, first in a picture, then in a story. For example, shown a picture of a crying boy with blood on his knee, they need to know not just what he is doing (surface meaning), but why he is doing it (implicit meaning). You may be surprised at how difficult some children find this! Stories call for more complex explanations: 'Why did the dog run away?' … 'Why did the man chase him?'

One effective way of helping children to understand the wider meaning of pictures and stories is by relating them to their personal experience. At first questions can be factual: 'Have you got a pet?' … 'Is your dog naughty sometimes?' … 'What do you do then?' Then you can begin to explore feelings and motivations: 'Has that ever happened to you?' … 'Did you cry?' … 'What did your mummy do?' … 'Why did she do that?'

Getting started Conversation skills **Listening skills** Narrative skills Discussion skills

12

Narrative skills

This step of the programme aims to develop children's ability to talk independently and extensively, at greater length, and without the support provided by conversation. As children move into Year 1 and begin to address the National Curriculum they need to develop more formal types of talking, such as describing events or activities, recounting experiences, retelling stories, explaining how something was made, or predicting the outcomes of actions or experiments. But while children get lots of practice in extended listening, they get much less practice in extended talking. They may be sitting listening for much of the day, but asked to 'give their news' barely once a week. Narrative skills need to be developed systematically. Although quite young children can talk about the immediate past, children as old as 5 or 6 still find it difficult to remember a series of events or describe them in sequence, and it may take some children all their primary years to establish sequencing skills, consistency in the use of verb tenses or an understanding of who is being referred to by a personal pronoun.

Narrative skills are crucial for literacy. Just as extended listening to stories or other texts prepares children for reading, so extended talk prepares them for writing. In order to write even a simple account they have to think of something to write about, put the events in the right order, mention the key facts and exclude irrelevant detail, and provide a beginning and an ending – with the added difficulty of having to turn all this into marks on paper or perhaps a computer screen. Since talking is easier than writing, they can develop these skills through such extended talk as describing a picture, retelling a story, recalling an outing, anticipating what is going to happen or explaining how to do something. '… speech propels writing forward. Pupils do not improve writing solely by doing more of it; good quality writing benefits from focused discussion that gives pupils a chance to talk through ideas before writing' (Ofsted, 2005). Children who find extended talk easy should take to writing relatively quickly, but children whose talk is less advanced will find the move to writing more difficult. If they cannot say it how can they be expected to write it? Boys, in particular, seem to show much more confidence in writing, and more willingness to attempt it, if they have been able to talk it through first.

Getting started

Conversation skills

Listening skills

Narrative skills

Discussion skills

Narrative also promotes children's thinking skills by helping them to develop coherent sequences of ideas. Children, as much as adults, learn to clarify their thoughts by talking them over, by thinking them through out loud. Narrative requires the ability to ask questions and to use verb moods and tenses. It develops children's understanding of time – of the past and future as well as of the present – and introduces them to ideas of possibility and probability, of what *could* happen or what *should* happen. These ideas are important for history, science and technology as well as literacy.

Children who have completed the *Narrative skills* step in the programme should be more confident in expressing themselves. They will be able to talk independently and at length about events, situations and objects, and to clarify their thoughts by talking them through or asking questions. They will be able to describe, predict and understand the differences between past, present and future, or between what is actual and what is possible. They will have more confidence in writing because they will know what to write and how to write it.

Initial screening (see Chapter 6)

Procedure

❖ Once children have settled into their new class staff should spend at least a week observing their spoken language in a variety of situations, both formal and informal, and focusing on the skills that are to be assessed.

❖ They should then complete the initial screen for all the children in their class or group. This should be done in discussion with colleagues, in pairs or threes or at a staff meeting.

❖ Each screen is divided into three bands, and children are assessed band by band. This means that if children do not have all the skills in Band 1, they do not need to be assessed on Band 2; and if they do not have all the skills in Band 2, they do not need to be assessed on Band 3.

❖ A skill should be credited only if a child is using it *confidently*, *competently* and *consistently*. If there is any doubt or disagreement, or the child's use of the particular skill is irregular or infrequent, it should not be credited. At this stage it is better to underestimate children's abilities than to overestimate them.

❖ Children who have all the skills in Bands 1 and 2 and at least one skill in Band 3 are identified as reasonably *Competent* in the relevant skills.

❖ Children who have all the skills in Band 1 and at least one skill in Band 2 are identified as *Developing* the relevant skills.

❖ All other children, that is, children who do not have all the skills in Band 1 and at least one skill in Band 2, are identified as *Delayed* in the relevant skills.

Note that children who do not have all the skills in Band 1 count as *Delayed* even if they have more than one skill in Band 2 and that children who do not have all the skills in Band 2 still count as *Developing* even if they have more than one skill in Band 3.

Getting started Conversation skills Listening skills

Narrative skills

Discussion skills

Using the skills checklists (see Chapter 6)

There are three checklists: *Talking about the present*, *Talking about the past* and *Talking about the future*. All three include work on verb tenses and relevant question forms. Notes are included for linking this spoken language work to early writing, starting with simple writing such as lists, notes or messages, then moving on to past tense and future tense writing.

Procedure

❖ Staff should work through each checklist in turn, focusing on just a few items at a time. Each skill should be made an explicit teaching objective for one or more weeks to ensure that staff focus on that skill with all children and in all relevant activities, across the day and through the week.

❖ This can be a rolling programme of three or four skills at a time. This means that the class starts with one or two skills in the first week, adds another one or two in the second week, then replaces one or two with new skills in the third week, and so on.

❖ The sequence of skills in the checklist is meant only as a guide. Intervention should also be guided by the skills that children are developing spontaneously. In teaching one skill staff will often have been introducing another, and this can provide an easy transition from one skill to the next.

❖ Staff may find it helpful to identify in advance the skills they are going to teach and the order in which they are going to teach them, and build them into their advance planning, so lessons can be prepared, resources gathered and support staff guided in their work with small groups or individual children. But planning needs to be flexible because some skills may take longer to learn than expected, and some weeks should be left free so that staff can go back and repeat or reinforce any skills that children have been finding difficult.

❖ A list of the skills selected for current teaching should be displayed prominently in the classroom so all staff can refer to them and encourage and reinforce them at all times during the day.

Classroom intervention

The general procedure is as set out in Chapter 6 but, for this step in the programme, partner work has proved much more effective than small-group work. It is easier to manage because it involves the whole class, and takes pressure off staff because it allows children to work on their own. It will boost the confidence and conversational skills of anxious or less able children, and give them the extra practice, consolidation and generalization it is otherwise difficult to provide in Year 1 classes. Children will enjoy and learn from it and it enables them to help and support each other as well as learning from the teacher, which is something our education system does not encourage often enough.

In fact, partner work has proved so successful that staff have found it becomes an important tool in all teaching, not just in language work. It can be used to deliver any part of the curriculum and soon becomes an integral part of normal classroom practice. Once children have got used to working in pairs staff can use it to consolidate almost any piece of whole-class work ('Now turn to the person next to you and …'). The *Narrative skills* programme provides a way of ensuring that children have the skills they need to benefit from this way of working, and it can then continue as a standard piece of classroom teaching in subsequent years.

Partner work may seem daunting and potentially disruptive at first, but staff should not be afraid to 'let go'. There tend to be two major concerns: that it will be too noisy, and that children will not stay on topic. These concerns have not been substantiated ('It's amazing what children can do when you put them to it!') Noise level should not be a problem if, for example, children are told to use their 'small' voice for partner work and their 'big' voice in whole-class lessons. They will also stay on topic provided the task is clear and appropriate, within their capabilities, and not allowed to go on for too long.

Procedure

Partner work

❖ The teacher should group all children in pairs, assigning each child a 'talking partner'. Any child left over can make a three, or be paired with the teacher or an assistant. The teacher should keep a close eye on any children identified as *Delayed*, and sometimes act as their partner.

❖ Partner work seems to work better if less able or more anxious children are paired with stronger or more confident children. Children identified as *Competent* and *Developing*, or *Developing* and *Delayed*, can be paired but it is not a good idea to pair *Competent* and *Delayed* children because the *Competent* children may dominate and not allow the *Delayed* children the practice they need.

❖ It may also be better, pedagogically and socially, for children to have different partners at different times or for different lessons. As they become experienced in this way of working, children can be allowed to choose their own partners, so long as they do not always choose the same one.

❖ All children in the class should have some partner work every day specifically on their narrative skills. The teacher should introduce each activity by modelling it a few times with children in the class, and say how long she is going to allow for the exercise – three or four minutes may be enough, especially at first. At the end of the exercise she should praise the class for working well together regardless of what they may have achieved but highlight any good points, such as not making too much noise.

❖ A good way of providing whole-class feedback is to have a 'hot seat': at the end of a partner-work session one child sits in the hot seat and tells the rest of the class what he and his partner have been doing.

Whole-class work

❖ The teacher should first explain to the whole class what partner work is, how it works and what the rules are (taking turns, listening to each other, etc.). She may need to repeat this from time to time until children are familiar with the procedure.

❖ At the start of each week she should use a whole-class lesson to introduce and explain the skills that the children will be working on that week. These can be

Procedure

highlighted as 'this week's special skills' so children know which behaviours are expected of them and what they should be looking for in each other. If children know what is expected of them they are much more likely to exhibit the behaviour in question.

❖ The teacher should also identify at least one occasion every day to feature specific skills or question forms chosen from those that children are currently working on. Talk-time, story-time and circle-time are obvious opportunities for developing these skills. She should work on the same skills over several days, trying to include as many children as possible, especially those identified as *Delayed* or *Developing*.

❖ All staff should be encouraged to use every other opportunity through the day to model, encourage and reinforce these skills with individual children.

Teaching method (see Chapter 6)

The following are the key techniques for teaching these skills.

◆ *Modelling*: the adult demonstrates the skill she wants children to learn, for example she describes a familiar TV programme or how she made something, and encourages them to do the same.

◆ *Highlighting*: the adult draws attention to the relevant skill by discussing it, emphasizing its importance, or explaining how, when or why we use it, for example she can discuss why we sometimes need to ask 'How?' or 'Why?' and what it helps us to find out. She can also do this by asking questions – 'What do we need to do when we tell someone a story?' – discussing the children's responses, and then summarizing and highlighting the key points: 'So when we tell a story we have to say who the people are and then say what happened, bit by bit, in the right order.'

◆ *Prompting*: the adult encourages the child to respond, directing him towards the appropriate behaviour: 'What happens next?' … 'What do you think that boy is going to do?' … 'Can you think of another ending?'

◆ *Rewarding*: the adult rewards appropriate responses with praise and further encouragement. If the praise can emphasize what was good about the response – 'Well done, Mary. You told James lots about that picture.' … 'Good thinking, William! That would make a good ending.' – it will help children to recognize what it is you want them to learn. If a response is not quite what the adult is looking for, she can encourage a more appropriate response by asking questions, prompting or modelling the skill again.

Vocabulary teaching (see Chapter 7)

The *Narrative skills* vocabulary consists of nouns, adjectives and a few adverbs that children will need to know in Year 1, selected from early cross-curricular vocabulary and the vocabulary of feelings and emotion. They will find it easiest to learn these words through practical involvement with real objects. Nouns can be taught by doing something or by making things (cutting out or handling *shapes*, measuring the *length* of something, getting things ready for *tomorrow*). Adjectives and adverbs can be introduced and explained using concrete examples and activities (a *prickly* hairbrush, squeezing through a *narrow* gap, saying something *quietly*).

Procedure

❖ Staff should identify 6–10 words for teaching each week as 'this week's special words'. As well as words chosen from current curriculum topics, they should include between two and four words from the *Narrative skills* vocabulary list. If children are finding some words difficult they can be featured over several weeks, or repeated at different times during the year.

❖ It will usually be convenient to teach a selection of words from the same category (quality, colour, etc.) at the same time, but staff should avoid words that are similar in sound or meaning (for example *width* and *wide*, *slope* and *slanted*) and contrasting pairs (for example *height* and *length*, *equal* and *unequal*), which some children will find confusing.

❖ The words for the week should be introduced and explained to the whole class at the beginning of the week, and displayed prominently in the classroom for reference by children as well as staff.

❖ These words should then be included and featured by all staff on every possible occasion over the rest of the week, in whole-class lessons, group work, one-to-one interaction and classroom routines. Children can support their own learning by being encouraged to consult the list of this week's words, look out for them in their lessons and reading, and use them in their own talk and writing.

❖ Towards the end of the week staff should monitor the learning of all children and identify any words that seem to be proving particularly difficult. Children who are slow in acquiring new vocabulary should be checked individually.

❖ The crucial test is that these children understand the word in question, whether or not they are using it (they may be copying other children). Understanding can be checked by asking questions, or giving instructions and seeing if children respond appropriately, while making sure they are not following other children.

❖ Any children who have difficulty learning new vocabulary can be put in groups of between four and six children for additional small-group vocabulary lessons. The words that they need to learn can be entered on a *Vocabulary checklist* (Appendix 2) and ticked off as each child learns them.

❖ Teaching each word should normally continue until all children in the group have learned it (in the early years this may take several weeks). It does not matter if children are learning at different rates; these children will benefit from the extra practice. But if one or two children are having particular difficulty they should not delay the rest. They will need to be given whatever additional support the school or nursery can provide.

Getting started Conversation skills Listening skills **Narrative skills** Discussion skills

Reviewing progress and moving on (see Chapter 6)

❖ Staff can keep a running record of individual progress by entering children's names on the checklist and ticking off each skill or word as each child acquires it. A skill should not be credited until the child is using it *confidently*, *competently* and *consistently*.

❖ Staff should also review all children at the end of the term or the beginning of the next term, to bring records up to date and possibly to reorganize pairs or move some children from one category to another. Talking partners can also be reconsidered when starting a new checklist.

❖ Ideally, teaching of each checklist should continue until every child in the group or class has acquired all the skills on that checklist. This may not be possible by the end of term, in which case teaching of that checklist can continue into the next term.

At the end of the year

❖ Ideally, all children will at least have completed the second checklist by the end of the year. Children who are still very delayed at the end of the year may need special provision, such as further small-group work in the relevant skills, either in their current class or by returning to the previous year's class for some lessons.

❖ If a significant number of children have not completed the second checklist, or have barely begun the third, it may be sensible to continue teaching the current programme into the first term of the following year, and not to introduce the next step until the second term.

❖ Staff should in any case liaise with staff for the following year and pass on the details of children who have not completed checklists, their likely progress, and any further support they may need.

Narrative skills

Initial screen

Child's name	Band 1			Band 2			Band 3			Competent	Developing	Delayed
	Will talk when spoken to but may not initiate conversation	Can name people and objects in pictures	Can talk appropriately about what they are doing	Talks regularly to familiar adults and children	Can say what is happening in a picture	Asks questions spontaneously	Can say what is happening in a story	Can talk appropriately about recent past events	Can talk appropriately about what they are going to do			
TOTALS												

Children who have all the skills in Bands 1 and 2 and at least one skill from Band 3 are classified as *Competent*.

Children who have all the skills in Band 1 and at least one skill from Band 2 are classified as *Developing*.

All other children are classified as *Delayed*.

Getting started *Conversation skills* *Listening skills* **Narrative skills** *Discussion skills*

Narrative skills

Talking about the present

Checklist 1

Child's name

Describing the present

	Can name people, objects and activities in pictures using nouns and verbs
	Can describe people, objects and activities in pictures, using adjectives, adverbs and prepositions
	Can describe other children and what they are wearing
	Can describe themselves and what they are wearing
	Can talk in some detail about a favourite TV programme or series
	Can relate stories or pictures to their own experience
	Can talk about the feelings or motivation of the characters in a story

Question forms

	Can ask *What's that?*
	Can ask *What's that for?*
	Can ask *Is it …?*
	Can ask *Who is …?*
	Can ask *What is/are … doing?*
	Can ask *Is s/he /are they …-ing?*
	Can ask *Where is …?*
	Can ask *Do/does …?*

Sequencing

	Can put a set of 3–4 pictures into the correct sequence
	Can tell a story using a 3–4 picture sequence
	Can explain why a sequence of pictures is the right one
	Can give a series of simple directions or instructions
	Can describe a familiar sequence of events in the right order
	Uses sequence markers like *now, then, before, after, next*

Getting started   Conversation skills   Listening skills   **Narrative skills**   Discussion skills

Narrative skills

Talking about the past

Child's name

Describing the past

	Can say what has just happened
	Can give a simple first-person account of what they have just done
	Can describe a recent event, for example what happened yesterday
	Can describe how something was made or done
	Can talk about what has happened in a story or a picture
	Can talk about what happened in a recent TV programme or a video

Question forms

	Can ask *Did ...?*
	Can ask *Was/were ...?*
	Can ask *Has/have ...?*
	Can ask *When?*
	Can ask *Why?*
	Can ask *How many/much ...?*

Sequencing

	Can retell a familiar story with help
	Can retell a familiar story without help
	Can tell the story of a recent TV programme or video
	Can attempt to retell an unfamiliar story
	Describes events in the right order
	Uses past tense correctly and consistently
	Can use pronouns correctly and systematically
	Uses time markers like t*he other day, once, yesterday, before*
	Can identify the key points in a past account
	Can begin or end a past account appropriately

Checklist 2

Getting started

Conversation skills

Listening skills

Narrative skills

Discussion skills

Narrative skills

Talking about the future

Checklist 3

Child's name

Describing the future

	Can say what is about to happen in a familiar situation
	Can say what is about to happen in a story or picture sequence
	Can give a simple first-person account of what they are going to do next
	Can describe what is needed to do or make something, for example in cooking or PE
	Can describe a familiar future event or activity, for example going home after school or what happens at the weekend
	Can talk about what might happen next in a story or picture sequence
	Can talk about what might happen in a favourite TV series
	Can anticipate the outcome of a simple experiment
	Can suggest possible outcomes for an unfamiliar story
	Can suggest a new or different ending to a familiar story

Question forms

	Can ask *Will ...?*
	Can ask *How?*
	Can ask *Whose?*
	Can ask *Which?*

Sequencing

	Can give an account of what they are about to make or do
	Uses the future tense correctly and consistently
	Uses time markers like *soon, tomorrow, next week, later, later on*

Getting started

Conversation skills

Listening skills

Narrative skills

Discussion skills

One Step at a Time © Ann Locke (Network Continuum Education, 2006)

Narrative skills

Vocabulary wordlist

Quality	Colour	Texture	Sound	Shape	Size	Quantity	Number	Space	Time	Movement	Feelings and emotion
clear	cream	furry	higher	cone	depth	almost	double	anticlockwise	afternoon	beat	brave
darker	purple	prickly	hushed	corner	height	altogether	even	apart	autumn	exercise	comfortable
heaviest	scarlet	rougher	lower	cube	largest	equal	odd	beginning	evening	fastest	feelings
hollow		smoother	softly	curved	length	fewest	quarter	centre	month	freely	glad
older				cylinder	longer	part		clockwise	morning	jerky	greedy
solid				diamond	narrow	unequal		direction	spring	quickest	lazy
				graph	shortest			edge	time	rhythm	scared
				hexagon	size			end	tomorrow	slowest	shy
				octagon	smaller			face	week		upset
				oval	thick			left	year		worried
				pentagon	wide			opposite	yesterday		
				pictogram	width			right			
				pyramid				row			
				rectangle				upright			
				slanted							
				slope							
				sphere							
				symmetrical							

Getting started Conversation skills Listening skills **Narrative skills** Discussion skills

Notes on Checklist 1:
Talking about the present

Most five-year-old children have a grasp of past, present and future and are reasonably fluent in the use of verb tenses, including irregular forms like *found*, *went* or *did*. But they are likely to be erratic or inconsistent in their use of tenses when talking at any length, and many will be poor at ordering events into a coherent sequence. This checklist aims to develop children's skills in talking about current events and activities before going on to accounts of the past or future. This does not mean that talk about the past or the future and the use of past or future tenses should be discouraged or avoided. On the contrary, any correct or appropriate use should be encouraged and praised. But the emphasis here should be on talk about the present and the use of the present tense.

Describing the present

This set of skills focuses on developing more expanded and detailed descriptions of things, including accounts of what is implicit in a picture or story.

The first three items are relatively simple, and should be well within the range of most five year olds. The second item asks them to identify things in pictures, using words as simple labels. The third asks for more detailed descriptions, using more complex constructions: not just 'a ball' or 'a car', but 'a big red ball', 'the car is going fast', 'he's fallen over', 'she's talking loudly', 'he's very greedy, eating all the sausages', etc. Children can then be asked to describe other children, or themselves. They may find it easier to talk in detail about a favourite TV programme or video than about real-life events. They can attempt to describe the plot if they want to, but at this stage it is enough that they can say what the programme is about or who the main characters are. Telling a story which involves the past comes later. Relating events to their own experience – 'Have *you* ever fallen over?' – can help children to understand what the characters in a story are feeling, or why they behave as they do.

The teacher may need to provide a series of 'pointer' questions to help children develop increasingly detailed descriptions: 'Who's this in the picture?' … 'Where are they?' … 'What are they doing?' … 'Why do you think they're doing that?' The same questions can be used again and again in different contexts and can be written out in sequence so that children can refer to them and follow them through when working in pairs. This may seem unduly mechanistic and repetitive but young children tend to be disorganized and unsystematic in their accounts of things, and learning to consider a series of questions in the correct order will help them to think and describe things more coherently.

For more detailed suggestions for small-group activities see the Activities Handbook in *Teaching Talking* (Locke and Beech, 2005), Chapter 6.

Question forms

The best way to teach questions is to select one at a time and display it in a prominent position as 'this week's question'. Although the question may change every week, the class can come back to the same one several times, especially if they find it difficult.

The teacher should first explain the week's question in a whole-class or group lesson, and get the children to talk about when they might use it, and what it helps them find out. That

Getting started Conversation skills Listening skills

Narrative skills

Discussion skills

question should then be featured in classroom teaching wherever possible, for example in circle- or story-time, as well as in partner work. It is also a good idea to have a 'questions table' with a variety of interesting and intriguing objects or pictures, which staff and children can use as a basis for asking questions. The teacher can use it to introduce the question of the week, and the children can use it themselves, in their pairs or at other times, to ask each other questions about the objects on display. The things on display may alter with the question of the week, and children can be encouraged to bring their own items to school to add to the table.

Note that the emphasis here is on asking questions, not on answering them. This can be practised in circle-time and partner work by getting children to take turns to ask each other the current question. It does not matter if they copy one another at first, asking each other the very same thing, until they become familiar with different questions of the same form. But it is important that they are not simply mouthing the words. They need to learn to ask questions as a way of getting information, so it is important that their questions get an answer, and that they listen to what the answer is.

The first three question forms – *What's that?*, *What's it for?* and *Is it ...?* – tend to overlap and can be taught and learned together. They are all about what things are or are like and can be introduced by having a collection of unusual things (or pictures of them) to talk about. Games like 'I spy' and 'Twenty questions', suitably simplified, are good ways of teaching *Is it ...?*

The next three question forms – *Who is that?*, *What is/are ... doing?* and *Is he/are they ...?* – are about people, and can be illustrated and modelled using pictures of people in different occupations, or people doing different or unusual things. They too will overlap, and can be taught and learned together.

Where is ...? can be taught by using objects in the classroom – 'Where is the blackboard?', 'Where is the door?', 'Where is the window?' – or by having pictures for children to ask each other about. *Do/does?* can be taught by taking it in turns to ask questions like 'Do you like ice-cream?' ... 'Do you have a dog?' ... 'Do you go shopping with your mum?' A variant which children may find more exciting is the game of 'Silly questions', where they ask each other silly things like 'Do you like spiders?' ... 'Do you eat flowers?' ... 'Do you go to bed with your shoes on?'

Children will find the second person *Do you?* easier than the third person *Does she?* but should be introduced to both forms. In circle-time, they can ask each other 'Do you like ice-cream?', 'Do you like swimming?', and then go round again asking 'Does Tracey like ice-cream?', 'Does Tom like swimming?'

For more detailed suggestions for small-group activities see the Activities Handbook in *Teaching Talking* (Locke and Beech, 2005), Chapter 5.

Sequencing

This set of skills focuses on children's ability to give a coherent, structured description of things or events in the right order. They will find this much more difficult than merely talking about them.

The best way of teaching sequencing skills is by using sequencing cards, that is, sets of pictures which tell a story when put in order. Children should first learn to put them in the right order, then be able to tell the story as they do so, and finally be able to explain why that order is the right one. This can be taught by deliberately putting some cards in the wrong order and seeing if they can say why it is wrong.

They can then be taught to give their partner a series of instructions, such as where to find or put things, how to play a game, or how to clean out the classroom pet's cage. 'Familiar sequences of events' are events that need to be put together in the right order, like what they do when they get up in the morning or go to the swimming pool, what happens at dinner time or a birthday party, or which way they go home (which route they follow). Once again, the teacher may need to provide a series of 'pointer' questions to guide the children in their partner work: 'How do you go home?' … 'Who do you go with?' … 'Which way do you go?' … 'What do you do when you get home?'

By the time that they can do all this, children should be using simple sequencing terms like *now, then, before, after, first* and *next*. But these may sometimes need to be taught explicitly, for example, the teacher can use group work or circle-time to ask what *before* or *next* means, to discuss the answers, and then to get children to give each other a sentence using that word.

Getting started

Conversation skills

Listening skills

Narrative skills

Discussion skills

Getting started   Conversation skills   Listening skills   **Narrative skills**   Discussion skills

Notes on Checklist 2:
Talking about the past

This checklist extends children's narrative skills into accounts of the past. They should not find it difficult to describe past events, but may have more difficulty in putting them in sequence.

Describing the past

The first few skills are again very simple and should be well within the range of most five year olds. 'Just happened' means the immediate past. 'Recent' means in the last day or so, depending on how memorable it is. Children may find it easier to talk about something that happened to or was done by someone else rather than to talk about what they have done themselves.

A good way of teaching these skills is to have 'review' sessions where children describe what they have done during the day or what they have just been learning. This reinforces their learning and develops questioning as well as their narrative skills. As soon as children are familiar with this sort of exercise they can do review work in pairs with their talking partner.

At this stage, talk about a story or a TV programme can be a general description. It does not have to be an attempt to retell the story.

For more detailed suggestions for small-group activities see the Activities Handbook in *Teaching Talking* (Locke and Beech, 2005), Chapter 7.

Question forms

Did?, *Was?*, *Were?*, *Has?*, *Have?* and *When?* all lend themselves to circle-time and partner work. The following are a few examples: 'Did you go shopping/watch *EastEnders*/have eggs for dinner?'; 'Were you outside/late for school/eating your lunch?'; 'Have you got a dog/read your book/been on a train?'; 'When did you go to bed/clean your teeth/see your grandma?' Some also lend themselves to 'silly questions': 'Did you eat any grass yesterday?', 'Have you got an elephant?'

Children will find the second person *Were you?* and *Have you?* easier than the third person *Was he?* or *Has she?* A good way of teaching *Was?* is to get children to ask questions about a familiar story: 'Was that a bad wolf?', 'Was Little Red Riding Hood scared?', etc. Stories can also be used to teach *Did?* – 'Did Cinderella have a pretty dress?', 'Did the prince find her?'

Why? can be taught using a set of pictures showing different incidents so that children can ask each other 'Why is the boy crying?', 'Why is the cat hiding?', etc. *How many?* and *How much?* are most conveniently taught in maths and science lessons or in practical activities like cooking.

For more detailed suggestions for small-group activities see the Activities Handbook in *Teaching Talking* (Locke and Beech, 2005), Chapter 5.

Sequencing

Retelling a familiar story, or retelling stories that are relatively new, is a familiar classroom exercise, but children may get more excited about telling the story of a favourite video or TV programme. The aim here is to help children to be more systematic and structured in how they do it, for example putting events in the right order without going into excessive detail, or providing appropriate beginnings and endings, rather than starting or ending in the middle of things.

The first four skills are simple narrative tasks. When children are doing these things in partner work, the teacher should be checking that they are putting the events in the right order, are using the past tense and using pronouns like *he, she* and *it* so that the person listening can keep track of who or what they are talking about. They should be able to keep to the right tense reasonably consistently and not be wandering erratically from the past to the present or even to the future; and they should have some idea of which pronoun to use and when they need to repeat the name of the person that they are talking about. They should also be using simple time markers like *one day*, *yesterday* or *last week*.

Teachers may need to work at whole-class level for some weeks before getting children to work on these skills with a partner. Once children are able to give a reasonably detailed account, staff can help them to summarize by asking what are the important things that happened. Depending on the example, they might ask: 'What are the clever things that boy did?' or 'What did the dog do that was difficult?' and so on; or they might just ask what were the main or most important things that happened. They should also check that children know how to start and to end their narrative.

Notes on Checklist 3:
Talking about the future

This checklist extends narrative skills into descriptions of the future. Children are likely to find this more difficult than talking about the present or the past. Most classroom activities provide opportunities to talk about the past and the present, but the teacher may have to devise opportunities to talk about what is going to happen.

Describing the future

These skills are relatively straightforward to teach but children may find some of them difficult, especially having to say what might happen, or inventing the end to a story. To help with this they should be given frequent opportunities during stories and classroom lessons and demonstrations to talk about what they think is going to happen, with the teacher suggesting possible alternative outcomes. They can also be introduced to anticipation games, where they try to guess what is going to happen next in a picture sequence or a story, and to discuss their suggestions with one another.

A pictorial weekly timetable in a prominent position in the classroom, with symbols or pictures to illustrate the different lessons and activities, can be a useful teaching aid. At the start of each day children can discuss that day's lessons and activities, first with the teacher, then with their talking partner. When they have got used to this they can talk about, not just what they are going to do, but also what they need and how they will start. This introduces them to planning as well as sequencing.

Question forms

These questions also lend themselves to circle-time and partner work: 'Will it rain tomorrow?' … 'How do you mix the paints?' … 'Whose is this shoe?' … 'Which is your bag?', etc. *How?*, *Whose?* and *Which?* can be taught using objects or pictures: 'How did he do that?' … 'Whose bag is black?' … 'Which car is the best?', etc. *Which?* can also be taught in science lessons: 'Which of these is the quickest/smallest/heaviest?'

Sequencing

The most important and most common form of future tense sequencing is planning a future activity. Children can be introduced to this by being asked to discuss something that they are going to make or do: what they will need, the order they will need to do it in, and so on. *Plan*, *Do and Review* is a useful exercise that can be part of any lesson, and part of most teaching. As well as reinforcing learning, *Plan* promotes talk about the future and *Review* promotes talk about the past.

From narrative to writing

Teachers are under considerable pressure to introduce children to writing as soon as possible, which may be before they are ready for it. Writing requires the ability to put your thoughts into a coherent form (narrative skills) and the ability to express those thoughts in the form of physical marks. Teaching tends to focus on the second ability and take the first for granted. But before they can write coherently and at any length children need to be able to talk coherently and at length. They need the vocabulary to express a range of ideas, they need the grammatical structures to express these ideas coherently, and they need to be able to remember those thoughts and put them in a narrative order.

Children who find independent or extended talk easy should be able to express themselves in writing with similar ease as soon as they have mastered the physical skills. But children who find independent or extended talk difficult will find writing equally difficult, regardless of whether they acquire the physical skills. They should not be expected to write about current activities until they can talk fluently about what they are doing, or to write about the past or the future until they are also able to talk fluently about them. Staff should always check that children show the relevant skill in their spoken language – telling a coherent story, talking about what will or might happen – before expecting them to produce it in their written work.

Moreover, independent writing often begins in the wrong place for many children. They are told to write a sentence or to write their news, but writing news is past-tense writing, which many children find difficult, and writing a sentence can seem a pointless, even meaningless exercise. Some children will not understand what a sentence is. It adds an unnecessary grammatical burden to what is already a difficult task, and even if they can do it, what exactly is the point? Adults seldom write a sentence just for the sake of writing one.

Systematic writing should begin instead with simple exercises that are enjoyable and meaningful and make as few demands as possible on children's grammatical and narrative skills. Obvious places to start include: names and addresses; labels for boxes, shelves or cupboards; lists of friends or family; what they want as birthday or Christmas presents; or what they want to take on holiday. These all allow children to use a new physical skill – writing things down – without making demands on their linguistic competence. The teacher can then introduce simple extended writing, like messages, directions and instructions, recipes, questions and answers, or notes to friends, followed by present-tense descriptions of themselves, their friends, where they live, etc., before moving on to news and stories. Children can use mini-whiteboards to write each other notes, messages or questions and answers, or they can be displayed on a class message or bulletin board.

The *Narrative skills* checklists will allow teachers to gauge the speed at which they can introduce various types of writing. Here are some writing tasks that can be introduced as children master the relevant narrative skills.

Writing in the present (Checklist 1):

◆ writing labels, lists, etc.

◆ writing simple texts, for example messages or notes

◆ writing the answers to simple questions like 'Who is this?' … 'Where are they?' … 'What are they doing?'

◆ writing simple descriptions of themselves, their family, the school, etc.

Writing about the past (Checklist 2):

◆ writing simple descriptions of recent personal experiences

◆ writing factual accounts of recent events, for example a school trip

◆ writing down a familiar story

◆ writing out a simple story of their own.

Writing for the future (Checklist 3):

◆ writing a simple account of what will happen, for example what they will do tomorrow

◆ writing a request for information or materials, for example for topic work

◆ writing a possible ending for a familiar or unfamiliar story.

These and other activities are described in more detail in the Activities Handbook in *Teaching Talking* (Locke and Beech, 2005), Chapter 10.

Getting started

Conversation skills

Listening skills

Narrative skills

Discussion skills

13

Discussion skills

Discussion can be seen as extended and expanded conversation. The rules are much the same: we have to take turns as speaker and listener, listen and respond to what is said, and either keep to the topic or change it in an acceptable way. But discussion usually goes on for longer on a single theme, and involves more people, with longer periods of both listening and speaking. So it also uses the skills of extended listening and extended speaking. Children may have to follow a line of thought, remember it while others are speaking, and then produce their own extended response. Discussion also tends to be more abstract. Whereas conversation tends to be about particular events and activities, discussion tends to be about ideas and arguments.

Discussion is a highly effective but under-used means of teaching and learning, more common in other countries than in Britain. Children, like adults, learn best if they learn for themselves, if they learn by doing, if they are active rather than passive. One way that they can do this is by talking about what they know, discussing it with the teacher or other children; by talking about what else they need to know, and asking questions to find out; then by talking about what they have discovered and reflecting on what they have learned. Discussion enables children to learn from other children as well as from teachers, and encourages them to find things out for themselves. It helps them to do this together, helping each other instead of having to do it on their own.

Discussion is also an effective way of developing children's thinking skills because it is, in effect, thinking aloud. Talking through something is often easier than silent thought, for children as well as adults. In discussion, children have to formulate their own ideas and opinions, and subject them to the judgment of others. They may have to clarify, explain or justify what they are saying, and at the same time consider other people's ideas or opinions, clarify and evaluate them, and possibly adjust or modify their own views in the light of what they have heard.

Discussion can also introduce children to exploring and debating ideas that aren't a matter of right or wrong, correct or incorrect, but a matter of opinion, where people can have

Getting started

Conversation skills

Listening skills

Narrative skills

Discussion skills

different points of view. Some schools have even introduced Philosophy for Children (P4C), not because they expect to turn children into mature philosophers, but because it provides an opportunity to express personal opinions, discuss more abstract ideas, and think through these ideas by talking about them.

Discussion helps to develop children's understanding of other people because they don't just learn from others, they learn about them. They learn about their interests, needs and wants as well as their opinions, attitudes and points of view. They learn to take other people's perspective, to understand and accept different points of view, and when different interests conflict they have to learn how to negotiate, reach agreement and, if necessary, compromise.

Discussion can also be used to develop children's ability to identify, describe and explain their feelings – to themselves as well as others. This is an important part of what is often called 'emotional literacy' – the ability to recognize, manage and communicate your thoughts, feelings and behaviour, and interpret and respond to the emotions and actions of others. These are difficult matters that we spend most of our life trying to understand but they are crucial for social living and children need to be helped to understand them at a level appropriate to their experience. It is increasingly recognized that schools should be giving more attention to this aspect of children's development. They are important social skills that take a long time to develop but need to be promoted in all children.

Children need to be experienced and confident in partner work and in the skills covered by the *Narrative skills* checklists before they begin work on *Discussion skills*, and especially on small-group discussion without adult support. If this is not the case – if, for example, Year 2 children have not done *Narrative skills* in the previous year – they should do the *Narrative skills* programme instead.

Children who have completed *Discussion skills* should be more able to think independently and direct and control their own learning. They will be more confident in talking with and to a group of children and, as a result, will have developed better communication, listening and social skills. They will be able to work with other children, and without adult support, to prepare, plan, predict, explain and solve problems. They will be more aware of feelings in themselves and in others, and better able to explain or justify their own behaviour or to give reasons and respond to the reasons of others. They will be willing to explore and resolve disagreements through talk.

Initial screening (see Chapter 6)

Procedure

❖ Once children have settled into their new class staff should spend at least a week observing their spoken language in a variety of situations, both formal and informal, and focusing on the skills that are to be assessed.

❖ They should then complete the initial screen for all the children in their class or group. This should be done in discussion with colleagues, in pairs or threes or at a staff meeting.

Getting started

Conversation skills

Listening skills

Narrative skills

Procedure

❖ Each screen is divided into three bands, and children are assessed band by band. This means that if children do not have all the skills in Band 1, they do not need to be assessed on Band 2, and if they do not have all the skills in Band 2, they do not need to be assessed on Band 3.

❖ A skill should be credited only if a child is using it *confidently*, *competently* and *consistently*. If there is any doubt or disagreement, or the child's use of the particular skill is irregular or infrequent, it should not be credited. At this stage it is better to underestimate children's abilities than overestimate them.

❖ Children who have all the skills in Bands 1 and 2 and at least one skill in Band 3 are identified as reasonably *Competent* in the relevant skills.

❖ Children who have all the skills in Band 1 and at least one skill in Band 2 are identified as *Developing* the relevant skills.

❖ All other children, that is, children who do not have all the skills in Band 1 and at least one skill in Band 2, are identified as *Delayed* in the relevant skills.

Note that children who do not have all the skills in Band 1 count as *Delayed* even if they have more than one skill in Band 2 and children who do not have all the skills in Band 2 still count as *Developing* even if they have more than one skill in Band 3.

Using the skills checklists (see Chapter 6)

There are three checklists. *Learning through discussion* covers the basic discussion skills, including using discussion to explore information and extend knowledge. *Planning and problem solving* also includes explanation. *Negotiation and emotional literacy* deals with agreement and compromise, and with children's understanding of feelings and emotion.

Some of the skills on these checklists are relatively simple but others are quite complex and many will be open-ended. They are skills we go on learning for the rest of our lives! Staff need to be particularly careful not to move too fast for the children in their class. It does not matter if the checklists are not completed by the end of a term or the end of a year. There is, in fact, much to be said for extending the *Discussion skills* programme over at least two years (Years 2 and 3 in England), though this may be difficult or impossible where children change schools between Year 2 and Year 3.

Procedure

❖ Staff should work through each checklist in turn, focusing on just a few items at a time. Each skill should be made an explicit teaching objective for one or more weeks, to ensure that staff focus on that skill with all children and in all relevant activities, across the day and through the week.

❖ This can be a rolling programme of three or four skills at a time. This means that the class starts with one or two skills in the first week, adds another one or two in the second week, then replaces one or two with new skills in the third week, and so on.

Discussion skills

Getting started · Conversation skills · Listening skills · Narrative skills · **Discussion skills**

rocedure

❖ The sequence of skills in the checklist is meant only as a guide. Intervention should also be guided by the skills that children are developing spontaneously. In teaching one skill staff will often have been introducing another, and this can provide an easy transition from one skill to the next.

❖ Staff may find it helpful to identify in advance the skills they are going to teach and the order in which they are going to teach them, and build them into their advance planning so lessons can be prepared, resources gathered and support staff guided in their work with small groups or individual children. But planning needs to be flexible because some skills may take longer to learn than expected, and some weeks should be left free so that staff can go back and repeat or reinforce any skills that children have been finding difficult.

❖ A list of the skills selected for current teaching should be displayed prominently in the classroom so all staff can refer to them and encourage and reinforce them at all times during the day.

Classroom intervention

The general procedure is as set out in Chapter 6 but this step in the programme uses small-group discussion for all children in the class. Like partner work in the *Narrative skills* programme (Chapter 12), this is easier to manage and takes pressure off staff because it allows children to work on their own. It will boost the confidence and conversational skills of anxious or less able children, and give them the extra practice, consolidation and generalization it is otherwise difficult to provide in Year 2 classes. Children will enjoy and learn from it, and it enables them to help and support each other as well as learning from the teacher, which is something our education system does not encourage often enough. Discussion work can be used to deliver any part of the curriculum and should quickly become an integral part of normal classroom practice. The *Discussion skills* programme gives staff a way of ensuring that children have the skills that they need to benefit from this way of working, and it can then continue as a standard piece of classroom teaching in subsequent years.

However, some children will find small-group discussion work difficult without adult support, and it may be necessary to spend several weeks at the beginning of the year – possibly even into the second term – concentrating more on whole-class or large-group discussion work, and introducing independent small-group discussion slowly by stages. It is also crucial that the discussion topics are kept very simple and well within children's capabilities, especially at first.

Small-group discussion may seem daunting and potentially disruptive at first but staff should not be afraid to 'let go'. There tend to be two concerns: that it will be too noisy and that children will not stay on topic. These concerns have not been substantiated. Noise level should not be a problem if, for example, children are told to use their 'small' voice for discussion work and their 'big' voice in whole-class lessons. Discussion groups will stay on topic provided the task is clear and appropriate, within children's capabilities, and not allowed to go on for too long.

Procedure

❖ The teacher should first identify a set of discussion topics to be used for developing skills on the current checklist. These can be drawn from the current curriculum or from familiar classroom or school activities or routines. Some topics may be better suited to planning an activity than extending knowledge, or more suited to explaining things than to solving problems. Sample topics for teaching each set of skills are given in the checklist notes.

❖ The teacher should then prepare for each topic a set of simple instructions or questions that most children in the class can work on without supervision. Because groups will have to work through these questions on their own, they should always be well within children's experience and competence.

❖ If the topic is 'Rain', for example, the questions could include: 'Why do we need rain?' ... 'What happens if it rains too much?' ... 'What would happen if it didn't rain?' ... 'What can we do with the water?' ... 'How can we store it?' If the topic is 'Caring for our pets', the questions could include: 'Why do we have pets?' ... 'How can we look after them?'... 'What should we give them to eat?'... 'Where do they sleep?'... 'How much exercise do they need?'

Whole-class work

❖ The teacher should start by explaining to the class what Discussion is, why it matters and how it works. She could say, for example: 'Discussion helps us learn; we can get ideas from other people; it helps you to think about what you know and what you need to find out; it also helps to solve problems and to avoid arguments; so you need to listen to what others are saying and wait till they are finished.'

❖ All this is worth repeating several times over the first few weeks, and at regular intervals thereafter, to help children to reflect on what they are doing in their discussion sessions, and how well it is working. When they get to problem solving, agreement and compromise they should be told that it's not about being right or wrong, it's about considering different suggestions and proposals and learning from them. But the basic idea of listening to others, trying things out, and adjusting their views in the light of the discussion, should be emphasized from the start.

❖ At the start of each week the teacher should use a whole-class lesson to introduce and explain the discussion skills she will be working on that week. These can be highlighted as 'this week's special skills' so children will know what behaviours are expected of them, and what they should be looking for in each other.

❖ The teacher should also introduce each discussion topic in a whole-class lesson. She should explain what the topic is and why they need to discuss it, and go through the list of questions or instructions one by one, explaining what she expects the children to do or find out. This will be illustrated by actually discussing the topic with at least some of the children in the class.

❖ If children are not ready for independent small-group discussion, whole-class discussion may have to continue for several weeks. Group discussion without adult support may have to be introduced slowly and by stages.

❖ When the class have worked through one topic, the teacher can introduce the next topic, and so on through the term. Some skills, for example planning and evaluating, will need at least two sessions – one to plan and one to evaluate. In

Getting started

Conversation skills

Listening skills

Narrative skills

Discussion skills

Procedure

that case the teacher should use a second whole-class lesson to go over what she expects children to do in the second session, for example they need to discuss how well their plan worked out.

Small-group discussion

❖ The class should be divided into groups of between four and six children. The size of the groups will in part depend on the space available, but four to a group is better than six, especially for less confident or *Delayed* children. These groupings can be varied from time to time.

❖ Children who are very talkative or domineering should be grouped together because they are likely to dominate the discussions and not allow other children the practice they need. *Competent* children may be grouped with *Developing* children, and *Developing* children with *Delayed* children, but it is not usually a good idea to put *Competent* children with *Delayed* children.

❖ For discussion work, children divide into their groups to discuss the current topic in different parts of the room. Each discussion session can last 5–10 minutes.

❖ Discussion work should be provided at least two or three times a week. Once established, there is no reason why it should not happen every day. Groups including children identified as *Delayed* should have some adult support for at least part of the time, and groups including children identified as *Developing* should have some adult support at least once a week.

Teaching method

The simplest discussion skills, such as taking turns, keeping to a topic, or seeking and giving clarification, are the same as for conversation, and should be familiar to children from earlier steps in the programme, though they now need to be able to use them in wider contexts, over longer periods, and in larger groups. But more advanced skills, like summarizing what they already know, individually or as a group, discussing the merits of a proposal, or explaining how something happened, may be unfamiliar and need to be taught explicitly.

The basic techniques for teaching these skills – in whole-class lessons or when supporting discussion groups – are, however, the same as for conversation or any other spoken language skill (see Chapter 6).

◆ *Modelling*: the adult demonstrates the skill she wants children to learn, for example she shows how to list steps in order, how to evaluate the success of a plan, or how to suggest improvements.

◆ *Highlighting*: the adult draws attention to the relevant skill by discussing it, emphasizing its importance, or explaining how, when or why we use it, for example she might ask 'What should you do if you don't understand it?' or 'How can you help Joe understand what you mean?' She can then discuss the responses and highlight the key points, explaining what clarification is and why we sometimes need to do it.

◆ *Prompting*: the adult encourages the child to respond, directing him towards the appropriate behaviour: 'Does that seem a good idea?' or 'Why don't you think it's a good idea?'

◆ *Rewarding*: the adult rewards appropriate responses with praise and further encouragement. If the praise can emphasize what was good about the response – 'That was a good clear explanation. Now I know how to make it!' or 'That was a good idea you and Steve worked out together.' – it will help children to recognize what it is you want them to learn. If a response is not quite what the adult is looking for, she can encourage a more appropriate response by asking questions, prompting or modelling the skill again.

If children are having particular difficulty in developing discussion skills they can be given more practice by being given time to discuss the current topic with a single partner, pairing each child with a more able child. They should have this extra partner work once or twice a day if possible.

Vocabulary teaching (see Chapter 7)

The *Discussion skills* vocabulary is divided into the vocabulary of discussion and a vocabulary of feelings and emotion. The vocabulary of discussion is further divided into verbs and some other words. These are all words that children will need to be able to understand for their whole-class lessons about the discussion topics, and need to be able to use in their discussion groups. The vocabulary of feelings and emotion consists of 25 words that children should already be familiar with from previous steps in the programme and 25 new words. These words will be particularly important in third-term discussion work.

As with other steps in the programme, the emphasis in vocabulary teaching should be on ensuring that children understand these words. Provided they understand them they should, at this age, have no problem in using them in their discussion work. However, at other steps of the programme staff are advised against teaching contrasting words (*quiet* and *noisy* or *good* and *bad*) at the same time. This still applies to the discussion vocabulary but not to the vocabulary of feelings and emotion, because some of those words will be familiar to children, and discussion work in the third term works with pairs of emotions.

The list of familiar feelings and emotion words is not a comprehensive list from previous steps in the programme but includes the words that are most likely to be useful in the third term. Many of them form natural pairs, either with other familiar words (*happy* and *sad*; *pleased* and *sorry*) or with the new vocabulary (*greedy* and *generous*; *silly* and *sensible*). Others have opposites that are not listed but will arise naturally (*comfortable* and *uncomfortable*; *kind* and *unkind*).

Procedure

❖ Staff should identify 6–10 words for teaching each week as 'this week's special words'. As well as words chosen from current curriculum topics, they should include between two and four words from the *Discussion skills* vocabulary list. If children are finding some words difficult they can be featured over several weeks, or repeated at different times during the year.

❖ It will usually be convenient to teach a selection of words from the same category (quality, colour, etc.) at the same time, but staff should avoid words that are similar in sound or meaning (for example *describe*, *discuss* and *disagree*) and contrasting pairs (for example *correct* and *incorrect*, *possible* and *impossible*), which some children will find confusing (this does not apply to the vocabulary of feelings and emotion).

❖ The words for the week should be introduced and explained to the whole class at the beginning of the week, and displayed prominently in the classroom for reference by children as well as staff.

❖ These words should then be included and featured by all staff on every possible occasion over the rest of the week, in whole-class lessons, group work, one-to-one interaction and classroom routines. Children can support their own learning by being encouraged to consult the list of this week's words, look out for them in their lessons and reading, and use them in their own talk and writing.

❖ Towards the end of the week staff should monitor the learning of all children and identify any words that seem to be proving particularly difficult. Children who are slow in acquiring new vocabulary should be checked individually.

❖ The crucial test is that these children understand the word in question, whether or not they are using it (they may be copying other children). Understanding can be checked by asking questions, or giving instructions and seeing if children respond appropriately, while making sure they are not following other children.

❖ Any children who have difficulty learning new vocabulary can be put in groups of between four and six children for additional small-group vocabulary lessons. The words that they need to learn can be entered on a *Vocabulary checklist* (Appendix 2) and ticked off as each child learns them.

❖ Teaching each word should normally continue until all children in the group have learned it (in the early years this may take several weeks). It does not matter if children are learning at different rates; these children will benefit from the extra practice. But if one or two children are having particular difficulty they should not delay the rest. They will need to be given whatever additional support the school or nursery can provide.

Getting started Conversation skills Listening skills Narrative skills

Discussion skills

Reviewing progress and moving on (see Chapter 6)

Procedure

- ❖ Staff can keep a running record of individual progress by entering children's names on the checklist and ticking off each skill or word as each child acquires it. A skill should not be credited until the child is using it *confidently*, *competently* and *consistently*.

- ❖ Staff should also review all children at the end of the term or the beginning of the next term, to bring records up to date and possibly reorganize discussion groups. Discussion groups can also be reconsidered when starting a new checklist.

- ❖ Ideally, teaching of each checklist should continue until every child in the group or class has acquired all the skills on that checklist. This may not be possible by the end of term, in which case teaching of that checklist can continue into the next term.

At the end of the year

- ❖ Ideally, all children will at least have completed the second checklist by the end of the year. Children who are still very delayed at the end of the year may need special provision, such as further small-group work in the relevant skills, either in their current class or by returning to the previous year's class for some lessons.

- ❖ If a significant number of children have not completed the second checklist, or have barely begun the third, it may be sensible to continue teaching the current programme into the first term of the following year, and not introduce the next step until the second term.

- ❖ Staff should in any case liaise with staff for the following year and pass on the details of children who have not completed checklists, their likely progress, and any further support they may need.

See also the section on implications for subsequent years in Chapter 8.

Getting started

Conversation skills

Listening skills

Narrative skills

Discussion skills

Discussion skills

Initial screen

Child's name	Band 1			Band 2			Band 3			Competent	Developing	Delayed
	Converses easily with adults and other children	Can join in a conversation with more than one other person	Can talk about recent events in some detail	Can keep to the topic	Can seek or give clarification	Can retell a familiar story	Can talk about what is needed to do or to make something	Can attempt to retell an unfamiliar story	Can talk about what might happen			
TOTALS												

Sidebar tabs: Getting started / Conversation skills / Listening skills / Narrative skills / **Discussion skills**

Children who have all the skills in Bands 1 and 2 and at least one skill from Band 3 are classified as *Competent*.

Children who have all the skills in Band 1 and at least one skill from Band 2 are classified as *Developing*.

All other children are classified as *Delayed*.

Learning through discussion

Child's name

Basic discussion skills

	Can join in discussion with other children
	Can respond appropriately to other contributions by questioning, commenting, etc.
	Can wait their turn
	Can keep to the topic
	Can seek clarification
	Can give clarification
	Can extend their own or other children's ideas
	Can summarize their own contribution
	Can summarize other children's contributions

Extending knowledge

	Can summarize their own current knowledge
	Can summarize the group's current knowledge
	Can discuss what needs to be found out
	Can discuss how to find it out
	Can report their findings back to the group
	Can discuss other children's findings (commenting, asking questions, or developing their ideas)
	Can summarize what the group has found out

Checklist 1

Getting started   Conversation skills   Listening skills   Narrative skills

Discussion skills

Discussion skills

Getting started Conversation skills Listening skills Narrative skills

Discussion skills

Planning and problem solving

Child's name

Planning

Can give an account of what they are about to make or do											
Can identify the tools and materials needed											
Can list the steps in order											
Can comment on other people's suggestions											
Can agree a plan with others											
Can discuss the success of the plan and suggest improvements											

Problem solving

Can say what the problem is											
Can join with others in exploring possible solutions											
Can join with others in evaluating suggested solutions											
Can discuss the success of an attempted solution and suggest improvements											

Explaining

Can describe an activity in sequence, step by step											
Can describe what a piece of technical equipment does											
Can describe what you do to make it work											
Can explain why/how something happened											
Can explain why someone did something											
Can discuss *Why do we ...?*											
Can discuss *What will happen if ...?*											
Can discuss what might or could happen											

Checklist 2

Discussion skills

Negotiation and emotional literacy

Checklist 3

Child's name

Negotiation

	Can describe or explain the problem
	Can describe the conflicting interests or points of view
	Can explain or justify differing points of view
	Can discuss possible solutions
	Can state and justify a preferred solution

Understanding emotion

	Can identify and describe what the characters in a story might be feeling
	Can identify and describe what another child might be feeling in an imagined situation
	Can describe their own emotions
	Can discuss thoughts and feelings with other people, commenting, asking questions, etc.
	Can describe the situations in which various emotions occur
	Can describe their physical response to various emotions
	Can identify the impact of emotions on their behaviour
	Can identify the impact of their emotions on other people
	Can discuss ways of responding to or dealing with their feelings

Discussion skills

Vocabulary wordlist

Discussion vocabulary			Feelings and emotion	
Verbs		**Other words**	**Familiar**	**New**
agree	prepare	atlas	afraid	affectionate
argue	search	contents	angry	annoyed
ask	settle an argument	correct	brave	anxious
change your mind	solve a problem	dictionary	comfortable	ashamed
check	suggest	encyclopedia	cross	bored
compare	summarize	false	excited	calm
concentrate	think about	idea	friendly	confident
contribute	understand	impossible	frightened	curious
co-operate		incorrect	glad	determined
decide		index	greedy	disappointed
describe		information	happy	enjoyable
disagree		possible	helpful	fair
discover		problem	kind	foolish
discuss		reasons	lazy	generous
explain		sure	nasty	hurt
find out		topic	nice	interested
guess		uncertain	pleased	irritated
improve			sad	jealous
investigate			scared	lonely
look for			shy	nervous
negotiate			silly	proud
notice			sorry	sensible
plan			surprised	tense
predict			upset	thoughtful
prefer			worried	violent

Getting started Conversation skills Listening skills Narrative skills **Discussion skills**

Notes on Checklist 1:
Learning through discussion

This checklist sets out the basic skills that children need to hold a discussion, and to learn and explore ideas together.

Basic discussion skills

This set of skills focuses on the mechanics of holding a discussion rather than the content. Discussion is a form of extended and expanded conversation. It uses the same basic skills, including turn-taking, maintaining a topic, and seeking and providing clarification, but children may have to listen to a single speaker for longer, wait longer to take their turn, follow an argument through several contributions, speak at more length themselves, and maintain a topic for longer than is normal in conversation. They may also have to give fuller accounts of what they think or feel, and explain or justify those thoughts and feelings.

Almost any topic will do to practise these basic skills, but the best place to start might be the topic of discussion itself, using questions like: 'Why is talking together a good idea?' … 'What can you learn from other children?' … 'Why do you need to wait your turn?' … 'Why do you need to listen carefully?' … 'What can you do if you don't understand something?'

Extending knowledge

These skills are about using discussion to learn. Children need to be able to summarize their current knowledge, and to share and explore ideas with others. They need to be able to discuss with each other what they need to know and how to find it out. Then they need to be able to bring this knowledge back to the group and share it.

These skills will need two discussion sessions per topic. In the first session children can discuss what they know, what they need to find out and how they can go about finding it. Then they need time to discover the information in whatever way suits them or the topic – with or without adult help; singly, in pairs or as a group –– before reporting back to a second session and discussing their findings.

Possible topics and questions include:

◆ finding out about wool, plastic, light, sound

  'Where does wool come from?' … 'What else do you know about wool?' … 'What questions have you got?' … 'What don't you know?' … 'How can you find out more?' … 'What new things did you learn?' …

◆ finding out about pirates, Vikings, the World Cup

  'What do you know about pirates?' … 'What do the other children in the group know?' … 'How many questions about pirates can you think of?' … 'Where will you find the answers?' … 'Who is going to find out?' …

◆ finding out about your town, where people work, how your grandparents used to live, what we need to be healthy

  'How much do you know already?' … 'What else would you like to know?' … 'How can you find that out?' … 'Where can you find it?' … 'What did you learn?'

Notes on Checklist 2:
Planning and problem solving

This checklist is about using discussion to plan and solve problems, and learning how to give explanations.

Planning

Children can be very impetuous; they tend to launch themselves into things without thinking. This part of the checklist teaches them to think through an activity – what they need to do and how they need to do it – before they act, and then gets them to evaluate their planning after they have done it.

Discussion topics for teaching these skills can be based around familiar routines or activities, or selected from curriculum topics. Almost any project or experiment can be the basis of a planning exercise, and cooking is certainly an activity where planning makes all the difference! Possible topics and questions include:

◆ making a model, birthday cards, biscuits, a scrapbook

'What do you need to do?' … 'What things will you need to do it with?' … 'Will you need any help?' … 'What should you do first?' … 'What will you do next?' … 'What will you do after that?' …

◆ getting ready for school, a birthday party, a class trip, a music lesson

'What are the things you need to do?' … 'Can you list them in order?' … 'Have you left anything out?' …

◆ preparing the classroom for routine activities, or for special events like a class concert, a party, a parents' evening

"What do we need to do?' … 'What things do we need?' … 'What will happen if we forget something?' …

◆ planning a project, for example a trip to a local wood to find out about flowers or insects

'What will we look for?' ... 'What do we want to find out?' 'How can we find it out?' … 'How will we remember?' … 'When we get back to school, what will we do with what we have learned?'...

◆ planning an experiment to compare weights, bouncing balls, ways of defrosting a bottle of milk

'What things can you think of trying?' … 'What apparatus do you need?' … 'What should you do first?' … 'How can you compare/measure the results?' … 'What did you find out?'

Problem solving

This section is about deciding how to do things. Conflicts, where people want to do different things, are dealt with in the next checklist under *Negotiation*. Problem solving, like planning, requires children to think about something before they launch themselves into action. They have to consider the options and evaluate them before deciding on a course of action.

Getting started   Conversation skills   Listening skills   Narrative skills

Discussion skills

These skills may need two discussion sessions per topic. In the first session children can discuss what they need to do. They then need to try it out, before discussing and evaluating the results in a second discussion session. Almost any practical topic from science, environmental studies, IT, etc. can be set, first as a problem to be discussed, then as an activity to be tried out and evaluated. Other possible topics and questions include:

◆ how to clean up if someone spills sand, water, milk

'What do we need to do?' … 'How can we do it?' … 'Which is the best way?' … 'How well will it work?' … 'How well did it work?' …

◆ how to keep a drink warm, catch a kitten/dog/spider without hurting it (or getting hurt) or get a cat down from a tree

'What do you need to do?' … 'What ideas have you got?' … 'How well will they work?' … 'Which is the best idea?'…

◆ how to mix paints to make orange or yellow, make a paper bridge for a toy car to drive over, keep warm in the playground when it's cold

'How can you do that?' … 'What are all the different ideas you've got?' … 'Which is the best idea?' … 'How well will it work?' … 'How well did they work?' … 'Which was the best idea?'…

◆ what to do if someone hurts themselves in the playground, loses their library book, needs to practise their reading

'How can we help?' … 'What do we need to do?' … 'How can we do it?'…

◆ how to stop children losing their gloves, wasting paper, running in the corridor

'Why does it matter?' … 'Can we help?' … 'What can we do?' … 'Which idea is best?'

Explaining

Explanation is crucial in education. If children are to learn they obviously need to be able to understand an explanation. But the ability to give an explanation, to explain something in terms that others can understand, is every bit as important, in all aspects of life. Explanation requires attention to detail and sequencing skills, and the ability to analyse a process into component parts and state them in order. It also requires awareness of another person's perspective, of what they need to know or be told, and what can be taken for granted. Barrier games, where children work in pairs with one child having to describe to the other something which the other child cannot see, are a good way of developing these skills in all children, especially those who find group discussion difficult.

The checklist covers several different types of explanation (what something is, how it works, why it happened and why someone did something) as well as predictions (what will happen if …) and possibilities (what could or might happen). It is particularly important to choose topics or things that are already familiar to children. They may also find it easier if you give them two or three different topics at a time first, to talk about in a general way, before getting them to go into detail on a single topic, for example about the order in which things happen or what might have prevented something happening.

Getting started

Conversation skills

Listening skills

Narrative skills

Discussion skills

Possible topics and questions include:

◆ how to get ready for school, plan a picnic, borrow a book from the library

'What are all the things you need to do?' … 'Have you left anything out?' … 'Which one do you do first?' … 'What do you do next?' … 'What do you do last?' …

◆ how to work a computer, a video recorder, a mobile phone

'What do you need to do?' … 'What order do you need to do them in?' … 'Have you left anything out?' …

◆ why something broke/how it got broken, why/how something melted or got burned, how/why a pet died, someone got hurt

'What happened?' … 'What made it happen?' … 'How did it make it happen?' … 'Could anyone/anything have stopped it?' … 'How?' …

◆ why someone fell over, was late for school, went to London

'Do you know why it happened?' … 'Would that have happened to you/would you have done it?' … 'What might have changed it?' …

◆ why we live in houses, clean our teeth, go to school

'Do you know why?' … 'What would happen if we didn't?' … 'How can you find out more?' …

◆ what will happen if it snows, the paint jars leak, the car runs out of petrol

'Do you know what will happen?' … 'How can you find out what will happen?' … 'What can we do if that happens?' … 'What can we do now to get ready/stop it happening?' …

◆ what would happen if the bell didn't go, the teachers forgot to come to school

'What difference would it make?' … 'Would it matter?' … 'What would you do?' … 'What would happen next?' …

◆ what could happen if you run across the road without looking, throw fireworks

'What might happen?' … 'Does it matter?' … 'What would you do/say?' … 'How can we stop it happening?' …

◆ what might happen if you go on holiday, go to a new school, get a new car

'What would you like to happen?' … 'What wouldn't you like to happen?' … 'What else might happen?' … 'Which of them do you think will happen?' … 'Can you make them happen, or stop them happening?'

Notes on Checklist 3:
Negotiation and emotional literacy

Negotiation, in the sense of working out a common course of action in a situation where people may have different needs or wishes, requires and develops an understanding of people's different points of view. Discussion can also be used to help children identify, describe and explain their feelings to themselves and to others. This is important for emotional literacy and the ability of children to manage their feelings, control their own behaviour and respond appropriately to the behaviour of others.

Negotiation

Coming to an agreement or compromise about what to do in a situation where people may have conflicting plans and interests is perhaps the most important skill we need if we are to live and work together. It requires being able to understand other people's point of view, and being able to modify your own position to fit in with them. Negotiation is also important as a way of giving children practice in explaining and justifying themselves, or giving reasons for their own attitudes and opinions.

The teacher should first use a whole-class lesson to explain that we sometimes have situations where people disagree because they all want different things, so they have to talk about them and decide what to do. She can give some familiar examples, such as sharing toys, making too much mess or noise, or deciding who should clear things away, and talk them over one at a time. She can, for example, explain why we need to share, what happens if we don't and what we can do if someone doesn't want to share.

Once children are familiar with these ideas, the teacher can explain that people sometimes have different ideas about what is the right or best thing to do, and we have to consider their views as well as our own. This isn't a matter of being right or wrong but of finding a solution, possibly a compromise, that everyone can agree on. She should also discuss the consequences of not being able to come to an agreement, and the problems this can lead to among children, adults and nations.

When disputes arise in the normal course of events, as they surely will, the teacher should discuss them then and there, if appropriate, and praise any positive responses or attempts to negotiate, without unnecessarily criticizing any negative or selfish behaviour. She can then go back to these situations in a whole-class lesson, when all children are present, but concentrating on how the problem could have been resolved, rather than how it arose in the first place.

Possible topics and questions include:

◆ what to do if children want to play different games, watch different things on TV, play with the toys someone else is playing with

'Why is this a problem?' ... 'What do you think should happen?' ... 'What should we do if some people have a different idea about what to do?' .... 'What should we do if we all agree about what to do, and then someone doesn't do it?' ...

Getting started   Conversation skills   Listening skills   Narrative skills

Discussion skills

◆   how to decide who should do an enjoyable or boring job in the classroom, like taking a message to another teacher, putting the reading books out, or tidying up after a messy lesson

    'Does it matter?' ... 'Why?' ... 'What would you want to happen?' ... 'Would that be fair to everyone?' ...

◆   what to do if someone won't play with other children, breaks another child's toy, is being naughty (stealing, swearing, telling fibs), finds something that's been lost and won't give it back

    'Why is this a problem?' ... 'What might happen?' ... 'What can you do about it?' ... 'What do you think should happen?' ... 'Is that being nice to everyone?'

Understanding emotions

The checklist lists a number of ways in which children might talk about their feelings and emotions: what they feel, when they feel it, how it affects their behaviour, how it affects other people, and so on. They may find this easier if they start by discussing the feelings of characters in stories, or what they or their friends might feel in various imagined situations, rather than actual feelings in real situations. Familiar stories or imaginary situations can be topics for the first few discussion sessions: 'Why did he do that?' 'What do you think he was feeling?' 'What else would he feel like doing?' 'How did the other people feel?' 'How would you feel if …?' 'What would you want to do?' 'What would be the best/right thing to do?' 'What would your friends do?'

Children need to develop this understanding of many different types of emotion, from basic feelings like pleasure, fear and anger, through to more subtle emotions like confidence, boredom and jealousy. The teacher should start by selecting simple emotions in contrasting pairs, for example *happy/sad*. She should introduce each pair in a whole-class lesson, explaining the emotions and the difference between them, and giving examples. She will probably want to accentuate the positive emotion, but children may identify more quickly with the negative emotion.

The teacher should then work through several different emotions in turn, setting the discussion groups simple questions like: 'What makes you happy?' … 'What makes you sad?' … 'When are you happy?' … 'When are you sad?' … 'Why?' … 'How does it feel?'

This should be done before going back to the beginning to set more demanding questions like: 'What do you do when you're feeling angry?' … 'What can you do about it?' … 'How does that make other people feel?' … 'What can they do about it?'

How far and how fast she goes will depend on how well children respond to these questions in their discussion groups.

Items on the checklist should be credited only when children can demonstrate the skills with several different emotions.

The possible emotions to be set as discussion topics are virtually limitless, but some core examples are:

happy/sad	excited/frightened
pleased/angry	proud/ashamed
surprised/calm	bored/interested
confident/anxious	friendly/lonely
loving/hating	enjoying/disliking
jealous/admiring	generous/greedy
indifferent ('don't mind it')/irritated	

Some of these may be unfamiliar to the children, in the sense that they haven't thought about them before, and may need to be explained carefully with familiar examples. How far the teacher goes into more complex or subtler emotions will depend on how well the children are dealing with them in their discussion groups.

Getting started

Conversation skills

Listening skills

Narrative skills

Discussion skills

Appendix 1

A summary of the development of language and communication from birth to 9 years

As explained in Chapter 2, *One Step at a Time* is based on a curriculum, not a developmental, model of spoken language. That is, it does not attempt to identify and teach spoken language skills in the order that children might normally develop them. Instead, it identifies key spoken language skills in terms of their importance for progress at school, and features them at the point where they are most needed for the school curriculum. For example, many children will develop good listening skills and even good narrative skills (for example confident handling of tenses) by the nursery year. But listening skills are particularly important for phonics and reading comprehension, and narrative skills are equally crucial for independent writing. So *One Step at a Time* features these skills, not when children might first be capable of learning them, but in Reception and Year 1 respectively, because that is when staff need to ensure that all the children in their class do have the relevant skills. The nursery year concentrates instead on the most fundamental skill – conversation.

Even so, staff may find it useful to have the following guide to average development, to help them to assess the progress or delay of different children in their class.

From birth to 1 year most babies learn to:

◆ recognize familiar people as a source of comfort, pleasure and interest and are motivated to communicate with them;

◆ use their senses to explore and manipulate objects, starting the process of making sense of the world and identifying things they will soon want to communicate about;

◆ attract and hold other people's attention through body movement, gesture and vocalization;

◆ co-operate and take turns in their interaction with other people;

◆ 'tune-in' to the speech patterns of the people around them and understand single words or simple phrases used in familiar situations;

◆ initiate contact with familiar adults and other children.

Between 1 and 2 years most children learn to:

◆ understand and respond to simple questions and instructions;

◆ produce single words and use them to indicate things of interest, identify needs, gain attention or share an interest with others;

◆ copy new words, and produce some speech sounds clearly;

◆ enjoy simple speech-action games like 'Round and round the garden', and join in the actions;

◆ identify familiar objects and actions from pictures.

Between 2 and 3 years most children learn to:

◆ understand and produce a steadily increasing number of new words (by 3 years most children are able to use several hundred words confidently);

◆ link words together and show some awareness of grammatical features by, for example, using pronouns (*I, you, she, they*, etc.) or verb tenses (*was talking, jumped,* etc.);

◆ have regular conversations with familiar adults and children;

◆ use language in different contexts, such as play, everyday routines (dressing, washing, eating, etc.) or talking about stories;

◆ produce a good range of speech sounds accurately;

◆ enjoy listening to and repeating simple rhymes;

◆ discuss scenes in pictures and follow simple stories.

Between 3 and 4 years most children learn to:

◆ speak clearly and hold intelligible conversations with familiar and less familiar adults;

◆ understand and use a vocabulary of several hundred to two or three thousand words;

◆ co-operate and converse with other children in a variety of play situations;

◆ understand and use adult sentences and grammatical features;

◆ use language for an increasing range of purposes, such as directing, asking questions, commenting and expressing feelings;

◆ repeat songs or rhymes from memory, and 'play' with words or sounds;

◆ contribute to talking about past events and discussing the future;

◆ use pencils, crayons, etc. to 'draw' on paper.

Between 4 and 5 years most children learn to:

◆ use conversation to co-ordinate behaviour with adults and/or children;

◆ contribute actively to imaginative play, for example by directing self and others through conversation, and taking different roles in group play;

◆ use constructions like *why … because* and *if … then* as a means of reasoning;

◆ talk about present, past and future events, and make a good attempt to retell a story, describe a recent event or talk about what they are going to do;

◆ listen with interest to stories and relate them to their own experience;

◆ 'read' books to themselves, possibly recognizing some familiar words in print, such as their name;

◆ enjoy games with speech sounds, such as clapping out the rhythm of words or phrases, recognizing words that rhyme or playing 'I spy';

◆ use pencils, crayons, etc. to draw pictures and to 'write'.

Between 5 and 6 years most children learn to:

◆ use language for an increasing number of educational purposes, such as observing people or animals, comparing objects, explaining, etc.;

◆ recount recent experiences in chronological order, and predict possible future events;

◆ appreciate that words can be written down, and show interest in having their own words written down or attempt to write them themselves;

◆ discriminate sounds in words and recognize that these can be written down as letters;

◆ read single words, at first in familiar, gradually in less familiar, contexts;

- begin to write words accurately from memory;
- work with other children to plan future activity and consider the equipment needed and steps required to complete the task.

Between 6 and 7 years most children learn to:

- work with other children to organize tasks and solve problems;
- follow a lengthy sequence of ideas in stories, make predictions about possible developments to a story, and give reasons;
- use language to negotiate and reach agreement with others;
- read simple stories, and answer questions about their reading;
- use their reading to acquire new vocabulary;
- tell a simple story or outline a sequence of events, prior to producing a written account;
- write an increasing number of words from memory and produce simple sequences of ideas in writing;
- use sound–letter links to read and spell unknown words.

Between 7 and 9 years most children learn to:

- plan and produce collaborative work in discussion with other children, for example a short story, a simple play, an account of personal experience, or a scientific or mathematical investigation;
- work with other children to identify problems and explore possible solutions;
- follow extended directions or instructions and long stories or factual accounts;
- discuss their own and other people's feelings and behaviour;
- discuss possible improvements to their own or group work, such as the use of more effective vocabulary or corrections to illogical or incorrect sequences of ideas;
- read independently for lengthy periods and use their reading to gain knowledge or find out answers to questions;
- write for different purposes, both imaginative and factual;
- know most of the rules of spelling, and use simple punctuation consistently.

Appendix 2

Pro-forma **Vocabulary checklist**

Child's name

Words

Appendix 3: Sample planning sheets

Listening skills, Term 2 — **Hearing sound and word patterns**

Week	Week's teaching objectives	Small-group activities	Vocabulary
1		Miss Polly had a dolly / The wheels on the bus / Mother Goose nursery rhymes / Music activities	
2	Can join in action-word games and songs / Can march in time to music	Miss Polly had a dolly / The wheels on the bus / Two little dickie birds / Music activities / Mother Goose nursery rhymes	Quality: dark (colour) old - plain - same (plus topic vocabulary)
3	Can join in action-word games and songs / Can march in time to music / Can recognize at least ten animals or objects by their sounds	The wheels on the bus / Two little dickie birds / This is the church / Music activities (using drums etc.) / Animal noises / Sound-making activities / Mother Goose nursery rhymes	Size: bigger - fat large - short (plus topic vocabulary)
4	Can recognize at least ten animals or objects by their sounds / Can do the correct actions in action games / Can clap in time to music and songs	Animal noises / Sound-making activities / Two little dickie birds / This is the church / Humpty dumpty / Music activities / Songs / Mother Goose nursery rhymes	Quantity: less - much nearly - none (plus topic vocabulary)
5	Does the correct actions in action games / Can clap in time to music and songs / Can identify an object or musical instrument by sound, out of two / Knows at least ten nursery rhymes by heart	This is the church / Humpty dumpty / Polly put the kettle on / Music activities / Songs / Sound-making activities / Mother Goose nursery rhymes	Number: both - half next - second (plus topic vocabulary)
6	Can identify an object or musical instrument by sound, out of two / Knows at least ten nursery rhymes by heart / Can clap out rhythm of a word or phrase / Can complete the rhyme, in familiar rhymes	Sound-making activities / Mother Goose nursery rhymes / Clapping games (children's names / nursery rhymes) / Miss Polly had a dolly / The wheels on the bus / Two little dickie birds / This is the church / Humpty dumpty / Polly put the kettle on	Time: always - before early - sometimes (plus topic vocabulary)
7	Repeat any items that are proving difficult		
Half-term			

Talking about the past

Narrative skills, Term 2

Week	Week's teaching objectives	Partner work	Question of the week	Vocabulary
2	Can say what has just happened Can give a simple first-person account of what s/he has just done	Talking with partner about: - previous lesson / activity - what they did at break / playtime / dinnertime	Did …?	Quality: clear – hollow solid (plus topic vocabulary)
3	Can say what has just happened Can give a simple first-person account of what s/he has just done Can describe a recent event	Talking with partner about: - previous lesson / activity - what they did at break / playtime / dinnertime - what happened this morning / yesterday	Was/were …?	Shape: hexagon – slanted – symmetrical (plus topic vocabulary)
4	Can give a simple first-person account of what s/he has just done Can describe a recent event Can describe how something was made or done Can retell a familiar story, with help	Talking with partner about: - what they did at break / playtime / dinnertime - what happened this morning / yesterday - what teacher did - what they did in art and design / PE / music	Has/have …?	Sound: higher (sound) hushed – softly (plus topic vocabulary)
5	Can describe how something was made or done Can retell a familiar story, with help Can talk about what has happened in a story or picture Can talk about what happened in a recent TV programme or video	Talking with partner about: - what they did in art and design / PE - stories/ pictures / TV, videos	When …?	Space: anti-clockwise opposite – upright (plus topic vocabulary)
6	Can talk about what has happened in a story or picture Can talk about what happened in a recent TV programme or video Can retell a familiar story, without help Retells events in the right order	Talking with partner about: - stories/ pictures / TV, videos - what teacher did - day's events / outings / activities	Why …?	Feelings and emotion: feelings – shy – worried – glad (plus topic vocabulary)
7	Repeat any items that are proving difficult			

Half-term

References

Alexander, R.J. (2000), *Culture and Pedagogy: international comparisons in primary education*, Blackwell, Oxford

Basic Skills Agency (2002), *Survey into Young Children's Skills on Entering Education*, Basic Skills Agency, Wales

Boyer, E.L. (1991), *Ready to Learn*, Carnegie Foundation for the Advancement of Learning, New Jersey

Crystal, D. (1986), *Listen to Your Child*, Penguin Books, London

Cummins, J. and Swain, M. (1986), *Bilingualism in Education*, Longman, Harlow

Department for Education and Skills [DfES] (2001), *Special Educational Needs Code of Practice*, Department for Education and Skills, London

Department for Education and Skills [DfES] (2003), *Speaking, Listening, Learning: Working with children in Key Stages 1 and 2*, Department for Education and Skills, London

Department for Education and Skills [DfES] (2004), *Five Year Strategy for Children and Learners*, Department for Education and Skills, London

Ginsborg, J. (forthcoming), 'Language and Social Disadvantage: the effects of socio-economic status on children's language acquisition and use', in Ginsborg, J. and Clegg, J. (eds), *Language and Social Disadvantage*, John Wiley and Sons, Chichester

Hart, B. and Risley, T.R. (1995), *Meaningful Differences in the Everyday Experience of Young American Children*, Brookes Publishing, Baltimore, USA

ICAN (2004), *Nursery workers' poll says 'Turn off the TV'*, www.ican.org.uk/news

Kelly, R. (2005), 'Education and Social Progress', address to the Institute for Public Policy Research, 26 July 2005

Law, J., Parkinson, A. and Tamhe, R. (eds) (2000), *Communication Difficulties in Childhood: a practical guide*, Radcliffe Medical Press, Abingdon

Locke, A. (1985), *Living Language*, nferNelson, London

Locke, A. and Beech, M. (2005), *Teaching Talking* (2nd edn), nferNelson, London

Locke, A. and Ginsborg, J. (2003), 'Spoken Language in the Early Years: The cognitive and linguistic development of three- to five-year-old children from socio-economically deprived backgrounds', *Education and Child Psychology*, vol. 20 (4), 68–79

Locke, A., Ginsborg, J. and Peers, I. (2002), 'Development and Disadvantage: Implications for the early years and beyond', *International Journal of Language and Communication Disorders*, vol. 37 (1), 3–15

Myhill, D. and Fisher, R. (2005), *Informing Practice in English*, Ofsted, London

National Literacy Trust (2001), *Early Language Survey of Headteachers*, National Literacy Trust and National Association of Headteachers, London

Ofsted (2005), *English 2000–05: a review of the inspection evidence*, Ofsted, London

Pinker, S. (1994), *The Language Instinct*, Penguin Books, London

Qualifications and Curriculum Authority [QCA] (1999), *Early Learning Goals*, QCA Publications, London

Snow, C.E. (2001), *The Centrality of Language: a longitudinal study of language and literacy development in low income children*, Institute of Education, London

TES (2004), 'From grunting to greeting', *Times Educational Supplement*, 30 January 2004

Webster, A. (1987), 'Enabling language acquisition: the developmental evidence', *Division of Educational and Child Psychology Newsletter*, 27, 27–31, British Psychological Society, Leicester

Woodcock, J. (2005), 'Latent meaning', *Times Educational Supplement*, 18 November 2005

Network Continuum Education – much more than publishing…

Network Continuum Education Conferences – Invigorate your teaching

Each term NCE runs a wide range of conferences on cutting edge issues in teaching and learning at venues around the UK. The emphasis is always highly practical. Regular presenters include some of our top-selling authors such as Sue Palmer, Mike Hughes and Steve Bowkett. Dates and venues for our current programme of conferences can be found on our website www.networkcontinuum.co.uk.

NCE online Learning Style Analysis – Find out how your students prefer to learn

Discovering what makes your students tick is the key to personalizing learning. NCE's Learning Style Analysis is a 50-question online evaluation that can give an immediate and thorough learning profile for every student in your class. It reveals how, when and where they learn best, whether they are right brain or left brain dominant, analytic or holistic, whether they are strongly auditory, visual, kinesthetic or tactile… and a great deal more. And for teachers who'd like to take the next step, LSA enables you to create a whole-class profile for precision lesson planning.

Developed by The Creative Learning Company in New Zealand and based on the work of Learning Styles expert Barbara Prashnig, this powerful tool allows you to analyse your own and your students' learning preferences in a more detailed way than any other product we have ever seen. To find out more about Learning Style Analysis or to order profiles visit www.networkcontinuum.co.uk/lsa.

Also available: Teaching Style Analysis and Working Style Analysis.

NCE's Critical Skills Programme – Teach your students skills for lifelong learning

The Critical Skills Programme puts pupils at the heart of learning, by providing the skills required to be successful in school and life. Classrooms are developed into effective learning environments, where pupils work collaboratively and feel safe enough to take 'learning risks'. Pupils have more ownership of their learning across the whole curriculum and are encouraged to develop not only subject knowledge but the fundamental skills of:

- problem solving
- creative thinking
- decision making
- communication
- management
- organization

- leadership
- self-direction
- quality working
- collaboration
- enterprise
- community involvement

'The Critical Skills Programme… energizes students to think in an enterprising way. CSP gets students to think for themselves, solve problems in teams, think outside the box, to work in a structured manner. CSP is the ideal way to forge an enterprising student culture.'

Rick Lee, Deputy Director, Barrow Community Learning Partnership

To find out more about CSP training visit the Critical Skills Programme website at www.criticalskills.co.uk